Prai

Your Happiness Connection

"This book is a beacon of hope for anyone struggling to find happiness. Reen Rose's wisdom and practical strategies will inspire you to embrace a more positive mindset."

—Marci Shimoff,
#1 *New York Times* best-selling author of
Happy for No Reason

"We live in challenging times where many people are feeling anxious and overwhelmed. Finding happiness in life, despite the challenges it offers, is at the heart of *Your Happiness Connection* by Reen Rose. The book is a treasure trove of inspiring stories and practical strategies. Happiness comes from within - your mindset and your approach to life determine how consistently you achieve it. This book offers you the tools to achieve and sustain happiness more easily. I thoroughly recommend it!"

—Gina Gardiner,
#1 best-selling author of
Thriving Not Surviving

"In this brilliant book, Reen Rose skillfully guides readers through the art of cultivating happiness, even in the face of adversity. A must-read for anyone seeking a more fulfilling life."

—Fatima Whitbread MBE,
two-time Olympic medalist

"In *Your Happiness Connection*, Reen Rose offers a refreshingly honest and relatable guide to help you build sustainable happiness. The actionable 'small-step strategies' at the end of each chapter make it easy for readers to implement positive changes and shift their perspective, even in the face of life's challenges. Reen's strategies are underpinned by research on the benefits of consciously focusing on being happy. I recommend this book to anyone who wishes to increase the happiness in their life. Who doesn't want that?"

—Pamela Thompson,
#1 best-selling author of
Learning to Dance with Life

"Your life will have ups and downs, whether you choose to be happy or not. It isn't a change in your circumstances that makes you feel good; it's a change in how you view those circumstances."

Reen Rose

Your Happiness Connection

Your Happiness Connection

60 Small Steps
For a Happy Mindset
When Life Gets Tough

REEN ROSE

Your Happiness Connection
60 Small Steps For a Happy Mindset When Life Gets Tough

Editor: Emily Swan
Cover Designer: RedSandCreative.com
Production & Publishing Consultant: GeoffAffleck.com
Author headshots: Story Catcher Photography

ISBN: 978-0-9939883-7-0 (paperback)
ISBN: 978-0-9939883-8-7 (ebook)

DOWNLOAD THE FREE COMPANION RESOURCE!

To help you get the most benefit from this book, take a moment to download the free companion resource. It contains an affirmation and a reflection prompt specifically designed for each chapter.

Affirmations are like self-fulfilling prophecies. They're short, powerful statements that when repeated often enough will shape how you see yourself and the world around you.

Reflection means to pause to consider and is the way adults learn. This means it's important to think about the words you read and how the lessons apply to you, if you want to become happier and more resilient.

The Affirmations and Reflection Prompt companion will provide you with invaluable support as you work your way through each small step.

Access your copy at **www.reenrose.com/FreeResource** or with the QR code.

For David

Contents

Introduction

When I tell people I specialize in helping the world to be happier, I get a wide variety of reactions. For the most part, they fall into two camps: one that believes my work is important, and the other that thinks my vision is unachievable.

In the minds of many, a happy life equates with one that never sucks. It's as if the idea conjures visions of Cinderella skipping and singing among the forest animals. In truth, you can go through problems, challenges, and deep darkness and still be happy. You don't have to live in a fairytale or have lots of money to feel great about your life.

Everyone has times when their life is tough. No one lives in perpetual sunshine. Regardless of whether you're happy or miserable, you'll still have hills to climb, difficult people to deal with, and deep holes to navigate around.

Creating a connection to happiness is about more than feeling good. Positive psychologists have proven that it brings with it many benefits. Including:

- A greater level of success

- Improved mental and physical health

- Stronger connections and support networks

- Living longer
- Increased motivation and engagement
- Becoming more resilient to challenge and change
- Experiencing less stress
- Having a stronger immune system
- Achieving more success at work
- Being more creative
- Improved productivity

Happy people recognize the benefits of climbing the hills. They view challenging people as an opportunity to improve their people skills, and are willing to jump over deep holes, knowing they can always climb out of them if they fall in.

It isn't what happens to you in your life that makes you happy or unhappy: it is how you react to those things. Happiness involves making a choice to be happy and then taking small steps to achieve that goal. If you're the impatient sort, you might think by taking huge strides you can reach a state of happiness quicker. Giant leaps have a place in your travels through life, but if that's all you take, you'll soon exhaust yourself. Small steps can get you farther in the long run.

Choosing one small action and then turning it into a habit is the secret to lasting change. If you don't know where to start, this book can help you learn to view challenges from a more positive perspective.

When I was caught in the rain the other day, I didn't bemoan the fact that I was soaking wet. I reminded myself that it could be worse: it could be snowing. When I lost my car keys, I chose to be thankful that I had a car to lose the keys to and was grateful that I had a spare set. These may be small shifts in mindset, but they build into a major change if practiced consistently.

Does that mean I'm always positive and cheerful? Far from it. I slide backward from time to time when life gets tricky, just like everyone else, but this happens less often the more I practice maintaining a positive perspective.

When a shadow falls across your path, try to see a purpose for the darkness. It might be an opportunity to learn something new about yourself, or a chance to take a break from wearing sunglasses. If you can find a positive reason for the challenge you're facing, you'll feel better about the experience.

Your life will have ups and downs, whether you choose to be happy or not. It isn't a change in your circumstances that makes you feel good; it's a change in how you view those circumstances.

This book is a selection of articles. They have a common theme but are standalone pieces. You can progress through them in order or randomly choose a chapter. Each one ends with a summary or major point called In a Nutshell and a small-step strategy.

My intention is to provide you with an array of things to think about, along with a possible action step to integrate it into your life. You can read as many entries in a sitting as you want, but for maximum benefit, I'd recommend reading one and then taking time to consider its content and the small-step strategy.

As a clinically depressed happiness maven, I know from personal experience that it's possible to increase your level of wellbeing regardless of what's going on inside or around you. Choosing to be happy is a gift only you can give yourself.

Everyone is going through challenges, but sometimes it can feel like you're the only one who's struggling. That's why I share stories from my life, thoughts I've considered, and situations I've observed. It can be very comforting to know you aren't alone.

I've anchored my work in evidence-based research as I'm fascinated by the science behind human nature. Increasing your understanding of your unconscious behaviors and emotions allows you to work with them rather than struggle against them.

Thank you for taking the time to consider the wisdom contained in these pages. I hope you enjoy reading my work as much as I loved creating it. Absorb everything that resonates, release anything that doesn't, and please share whatever you feel someone else needs to hear.

ONE

Your Life's Purpose is to be Happy

Happiness is the meaning and purpose of life, the whole aim and the end of human existence.

\- Aristotle

Even before I thought of myself as a happiness maven, I agreed with this sentiment wholeheartedly. Who doesn't want happiness for themselves and their loved ones? I've spoken with many parents over the years, and when I ask them what they want most for their children, happiness is by far the most frequently given response.

Aristotle was a philosopher. He understood the importance of being happy for physical, emotional, and mental well-being. Today, this idea isn't just a philosophical notion. There's scientific evidence to support it. The benefits of being happy include having an improved immune system, stronger heart, and greater resilience to stress. There are even studies that show people who consider themselves to be happy can experience less pain.

But how do you go about becoming happier? Depending on what your starting point is, that goal may seem like a distant dream.

If practicing happiness is new for you, I recommend you focus your attention on the following trio of happiness boosters.

Gratitude

This is a cornerstone for boosting your feelings of wellbeing. Consciously take a moment to express gratitude throughout your day. Set an intention to notice at least three things that make you feel good when they occur. If you enjoy a morning cup of coffee or tea, take a minute to notice how the first sip tastes rather than gulping it down unconsciously. Thank your tastebuds for being so astute, or your job for providing you with your beverage and the comfy chair you're sitting in while you enjoy it. This action encourages you to live in the moment, which is a practice that has been proven to increase wellbeing. Try to experience those feelings of gratitude deep in your body.

If you realize at the end of the day that you've forgotten to do this, don't despair. End of the day gratitude is equally beneficial. Think of at least three things you're thankful for before you go to sleep.

Acceptance

You may think your life sucks, but don't agonize over things you can't change. There are many things you can't control. Accept this fact with compassion and shift your focus away from the areas of your life that you not only don't like, but also can't change. Take the time to discern what is, and what isn't, within your control.

Accept past decisions that cause shame or regret with as much grace as you can muster. One of my favorite sayings is, "It seemed like a good idea at the time." Remind yourself of this when things turn out differently than you'd hoped. Few people set out to purposely make a bad decision. With so many variables at play when it comes to decisions, there's rarely a guaranteed outcome.

Growth

Develop the attitude of a life-long learner and view your world through the eyes of curiosity. Learning opportunities are frequently hidden in the guise of challenges and seemingly wrong decisions. You learn more from your mistakes than when things work out easily.

Stepping out of your comfort zone to try something new is a great place to experience growth. Consciously look for new experiences. Be grateful for all the opportunities that come your way and get in the habit of saying yes to them rather than letting fear stop you.

In a Nutshell

Evidence-based research shows that gratitude, acceptance, and personal growth are all instrumental in boosting your wellbeing. Increasing their presence in your life is a good starting point for your practice of connecting to happiness.

Small-step Strategy

Choose one of the Happiness Triad strategies. Think of one thing you can do to make it more prevalent in your daily life. Don't rush yourself. Take your time to become comfortable with it before moving onto another one.

TWO

Create Happiness Habits

About half of everything you do during any particular day is habitual. That means you do it automatically with a minimal amount of conscious thought. My day usually starts with coffee. I may consider how much I'm going to enjoy my first sip, but I rarely stop to ponder whether or not I should make it or think about the steps involved in its creation.

Mindfulness is an important part of connecting to happiness, but there are times when habits serve you more. This is especially true if you want to make some lasting changes. Perhaps you'd like to adopt a healthier lifestyle or be less dependent on your phone. Developing some supportive habits could be just what you need to make intentions like these come true.

Humans have a limited amount of willpower. If you count on determination to get you off the couch and to the gym, you may find yourself giving up before your desired goal is realized. You can increase your chances of success by creating a few helpful habits.

Let me share three things you can do to increase your likelihood of turning a conscious behavior into a habit.

Stack your habits

Make a list of some of the habits you already have. This could include brushing your teeth, eating regular meals, or going to work. Attach your new behavior to an existing one.

Have a glass of water before or after every meal. Do some squats while you brush your teeth. Park further away from the office to get a few extra steps in. Adding to an already existing behavior can give your new one a much-needed boost towards success.

Give your action consistency

Having a consistent context – like a specific time of day – is a great way to increase your chances of success when it comes to forming habits. Go for a walk first thing every morning or stop at the gym on your way home from work. Set an alarm on your phone to remind you to move every hour.

Involve others

If you decide to go to the gym, play pickleball, or swim regularly, find a buddy to keep you company. You're less likely to miss your sessions when you know there's somebody expecting to see you there.

It's hard to say how long it'll take to turn your action into a habit. That depends on you as an individual, the behavior you're trying to ingrain, and the number of interruptions you experience.

Sixty-six days is commonly considered to be the time needed to make an action habitual, but don't get discouraged if it takes longer. That's only an average. Research shows it can take anywhere from 18 to 254 days for a habit to be formed.

Happiness is boosted by breaking free of mindless actions and living more consciously, but that doesn't mean you should abandon all your routines or automatic behaviors. It's about finding balance. Afterall, making exercise a habit doesn't mean you can't stop to smell the roses while you're there.

In a Nutshell

Habits are your brain's way of conserving energy. If you had to consciously consider every single thing you do during the day, you'd soon be exhausted. That's the upside to habits, but as with most things, they also have a downside. Automatic behavior doesn't boost your level of happiness the way consciously living in the moment does. The challenge is to find balance. Mix your habits with moments of mindfulness.

Small-step Strategy

Choose an action that you'd like to become habitual. For example, you may want to aim for 10,000 steps in a day. Start by stacking some steps onto an existing behavior. March in place while you brush your teeth, or while you wait for your coffee to brew.

For an additional boost, consider how you can add a moment of conscious thought to your habit. Choose a different exercise to perform when you brush your teeth, or vary walking in place with marching up and down the hallway.

THREE

Live from the Inside-Out

"If I get that new job, then I'll be happy."

"Buying that sporty new car will make me feel young again."

"A new partner will change everything and make my life worthwhile."

"I'd better buy a lottery ticket, because I need more money to make my life good."

These statements are all examples of living from the outside-in. You think that by changing your circumstances, you'll change how you feel about yourself and your life. If you believe happiness comes from any of the above statements or something similar, you may be disappointed, especially if you want to connect with long-term happiness.

Humans have an astonishing capacity to adapt to situations that spark extreme emotions. Take lottery winners, for example. Research shows that subjects experienced an initial burst of excitement, but within six months were back to their pre-win level of happiness. This was true even if the amount they'd won was enough to change their life dramatically.

Working to change your circumstances isn't the key to happiness. Altering how you feel on the inside is. Do this by getting to know, love, and accept yourself. Learn to embrace your warts just as enthusiastically as you do your beauty marks. What you buy or achieve makes very little difference to how happy you feel over an extended period of time. Remind yourself that your intentional choices and mindset are the key to living an emotionally satisfying life, not your circumstances.

In a Nutshell

How well do you know yourself? I'm talking about your authentic self, not the person you think you should be. Happy people know they aren't perfect, because there isn't any such thing. Instead, they see themselves as a work in progress. Knowing and accepting who you are at your core is the cornerstone for personal growth.

Small-step Strategy

Begin a reflection practice. You can journal your thoughts, or simply take conscious note of them. Ask yourself questions like:

- What are my favorite activities?
- How do I feel? What's contributing to that emotion?
- Who do I love spending time with?
- Where would I go if I could choose any destination?

Be as honest with yourself as you can as you think about your answers. Let go of both judgement and societal expectations. There are no right or wrong answers.

FOUR

Emotions are Fleeting

I was driving down the road the other day when I noticed intensely positive emotions bubbling to the surface. I could feel butterflies building in my stomach. I decided to lean into these sensations and enjoy them because I knew they wouldn't last.

When I was younger, this idea used to distress me. I wanted to enjoy these euphoric feelings all the time, but I knew from experience that wouldn't happen. I'd caution myself not to let my emotions get too intense. The higher my happiness, the greater the impending fall.

This may be something you can relate to. Humans have a wide range of emotions that fluctuate regularly. Just when you think you couldn't be happier, something happens to bring you back down to Earth, sometimes with an almighty thud.

You might find it helpful to understand that people aren't designed to be ecstatically happy for more than short periods of time. Your number one drive as a human is to survive. Having a range of emotions helps you do that.

Think back to a time when you felt over the moon. Maybe you'd just got engaged, won an award, or achieved a goal you'd been working towards for years. Was it easy to settle down and get your work done? Emotional highs make it hard to stay on task, because your mind is preoccupied with your success and ways you can celebrate.

In contrast, negative emotions are designed to raise your alarm system and get you ready for a fight/flight/freeze response. The minute your brain thinks you're in a win-lose situation, it makes a split-second decision. It chooses the strategy it believes will give you the greatest chance of surviving the perceived threat. This is also not an ideal place to be if you've got work to do.

The best type of emotions to have if you want to grow and get stuff done is moderately positive. This is the perfect mindset for problem-solving, calculated risk-taking, and creating lasting relationships as well as encouraging tolerance, creativity, and opening yourself up to new ideas and experiences.

Because it serves you to spend most of your time in this moderate level of feeling good, the human brain has developed something called "hedonic adaptation." Whenever you dip or soar out of your optimum range of happiness, it flares into action to pull you back into what's known as your "setpoint." This is the best place to be for connection and growth.

Although the word "setpoint" might make you think it's one specific intensity of happiness, it actually refers to a range of emotions.

A burst of intense happiness or a dip into negative emotions pushes you out of your setpoint, so hedonic adaptation pulls you back to your optimum happiness level so you can continue to grow and move forward.

You might think it's unfair to be pulled out of your ultra happy place, but remember it isn't a one-way street. Not only does hedonic adaptation drag you back from intensely positive emotions, it also helps prevent you from falling into a never-ending bout of depression, fear, or unhappiness.

Unless you're suffering from a mood disorder or other type of mental condition, at some point, hedonic adaptation will swoop in like a superhero and rescue you from your negative emotions. This is one reason you may feel much better after a good night's sleep.

It doesn't matter how far you stray from your predetermined normal range or setpoint, your brain will work tirelessly to bring you back to what it believes is the best place for your survival.

Research suggests that no matter what circumstances you encounter in your life, you'll adjust to them, and your emotions will gradually return to whatever's normal for you. This includes a major lottery win or an unwanted health condition.

Being aware that this cycle exists can be very comforting. When you notice it springing into action, remind yourself that it's a survival mechanism that's helping you live your best life, rather than simply another example of how difficult your life is.

As distinguished professor of psychology Sonja Lyubomirsky describes it, heightened levels of happiness and sadness are like puddles that gradually evaporate, leaving you back where you were before it rained.

In a Nutshell

Hedonic adaptation may not seem like a good strategy when you first find out about it, but it prevents you from standing still. Rather than getting stuck in a fight/flight/freeze response, or an intensely happy glow, it encourages you to grow and move forward with your life by changing your intense emotions to moderate ones. This is the best place to be if you want to grow.

Small-step Strategy

The next time you notice that your feelings are extreme, remind yourself about hedonic adaptation. It exists for a reason. It's helping you live your best life and allowing you to continue to move forward.

If extreme emotions don't seem to wane, consider speaking to your doctor or other specialist.

FIVE

Release Negative Emotions

I consider myself to be a positive person, but that doesn't mean I am always happy, or that I couldn't be happier. Let's get real about happiness.

You're programed to have a range of emotions. Negative emotions help during moments of threat, and mild to moderately positive ones help us grow and learn. It isn't wrong to feel unhappy, but it isn't the best place to spend most of your time. To help you move out of negativity, acknowledge your negative emotions and then let them go.

If they're reluctant to leave, try labeling them. I'm not suggesting you call them Clive or Cindy. Instead, look for the most accurate word or words you can find to describe them. Research shows that labelling your negative feelings is an effective way to reduce their intensity. In one study, participants were shown photos of people with emotional facial expressions. This triggered the amygdala area of their brains causing them to feel similar emotions themselves. This phenomenon is known as emotional contagion, and is one of the reasons humans feel empathy for others. When you look at an unhappy person, you tend to feel unhappy.

The subjects were then asked to name the emotions they were feeling. This simple act reduced the activity in the amygdala, lessening the impact and intensity of how they were feeling. So, the next time you find yourself immersed in emotions you don't want, try acknowledging and naming them, and then consciously letting them go.

In a Nutshell

Happy people don't pretend they're impervious to negativity. They try to choose environments that are positive and keep their minds focused on good things, but they have negative emotions, too. What separates positive and negative people is how they choose to deal with unhappiness.

Small-step Strategy

If you notice your emotions dipping, rather than ignoring them, acknowledge your feelings. Let them bubble to the surface. Suppressing negative emotions isn't healthy. The trick is to limit the amount of time you stay in this place. Try setting the timer on your phone for 10 minutes. Lean into all those negative feelings, but when the time is up, be willing to let your emotions go.

SIX

Why You Resist Change

I recently heard about a new way of packaging shampoo and conditioner. Rather than having liquid in a bottle, you can buy it in a bar like soap. What a great idea, especially if you're traveling only with carry-on where your liquids are limited.

I mentioned this product to a friend and was surprised at her negative reaction. Perhaps it caught my attention because she's a hair stylist who loves to travel. I expected her to at least be open to the idea.

She had lots of reasons to justify her opinions and they were probably all valid, although she'd never tried this new type of shampoo. That wasn't what interested me. I realized I was observing outdated programing in action. Humans have been programed from evolutionary times to embrace certain behaviors that helped them survive. One of these is a distrust of anything new.

If you try a bar of shampoo and don't like it, you probably won't lose anything but the cost of your purchase. People in more primitive times had too much at stake to try something new for the sake of curiosity. If they had tools and strategies that worked, they were better off sticking with them. If you tried something new to evade a predator or get food and it didn't work, there is every chance you would die.

Historically, change happened slowly. The same types of tools and strategies were used until they didn't work anymore and there was no choice but to find new ones. Change no longer happens slowly.

In the lifetime of my grandfather, he went from horse and buggies to cars; from slates to computers; from the moon being a mysterious thing in the sky to seeing a man land on it. Staying secure by maintaining the old way of doing things no longer works. Your world is changing so quickly that, if you slow down, you will be left behind.

Here are three ways to become less resistant to change.

- Recognize that resistance may be your 'go to' response. Notice when this happens and then open your mind by looking for reasons why this change may be good.

- Take time to explore both sides of any situation.

- Try new things on a regular basis. This will make you more comfortable when you find yourself pushed into change.

In a Nutshell

With the right mindset, you can view new things with curiosity, rather than fear. This is a vital skill if you want to foster a happiness connection. In our fast-changing world, it will serve you and help tame your outdated programing.

Small-step Strategy

The next time you're presented with a new idea, process, or activity, rather than refusing to accept it, try to have an open mind. View it as an experiment. Be curious. You don't have to love it but know that having first-hand understanding of a new concept or situation gives you an advantage and will lead to better decisions.

SEVEN

You Create Your Reality

One of the biggest adjustments I had to make when I moved into one of my former homes was getting used to the road noise. The sounds were distracting, and my dog was exhausted by all the extra barking he felt compelled to do. But in a very short time, we adjusted.

We began to barely notice the cars, unless there was a siren or loud screeching of brakes. This was true even when we were outside. Had the traffic become quieter, or less frequent? Not at all. If anything, at certain times of the day, it became busier than ever. So, if the noise was still there, why didn't we notice it?

Your brain is bombarded 24/7 with signals from your senses. Your eyes take in everything they see. Your skin feels anything it meets and continues to feel it until the connection is removed. Your nose registers the strong and subtle scents that surround you. Your ears detect every sound that comes within range. If you're eating or drinking, your tongue is assaulted by a myriad of tastes and textures.

Your brain receives all these sensations. It knows that your clothes are touching specific parts of your skin, and that your eyes see the spider scuttling across the floor. Why does your conscious mind miss so many things that your brain is aware of?

If your brain shared every message it received, you'd be overwhelmed. Being overwhelmed isn't much fun. It's like drowning, or being buried under more than you believe you can handle. You wouldn't be able to sleep, or focus.

To prevent this from happening, your brain uses selective filtering. This is also known as selective attention. Your brain processes only a small portion of the stimuli it receives. Your attention is drawn to the things your mind believes will help you survive, or that support your conscious or subconscious beliefs. Your brain likes consistency. It wants to support you in whatever you believe. It has no interest in confusing you or sending you mixed signals.

If you think money is hard to come by and only a lucky few get to acquire it, your brain will work hard to find evidence that strengthens that idea. It's the ultimate spin doctor. It will scan through the stimuli it receives to see what's appropriate to send you. It'll add an extra layer of support by interpreting these messages in whatever way helps strengthen your existing beliefs.

In Dr. Richard Wiseman's research on luck, he put his unwitting subjects into a situation where they walked past a five-pound note that was lying on the ground. Each brain received a message alerting it to the existence of the money. The difference wasn't in the stimulus, but in the selective filtering processes.

A desire to provide evidence to prove a belief in luck, or a lack of it, determined who received conscious awareness of the money. The people who self-identified as lucky noticed it. Those who believed they were unlucky didn't. It brings a whole new meaning to creating your own reality.

This isn't the first time I've written on the topic of selective information processing, but this time I want to throw a twist into the mix by suggesting you get proactive.

If you want to change your outer life, you have to start by changing your inner one.

Regardless of what happens, pessimists are going to see things negatively. Optimists will interpret positively. Possibility-ists will see possibility.

Do you want to be richer, or in a loving relationship? Maybe you want to work less but maintain your current lifestyle. Taking on a second job, joining more dating apps, or transitioning to a part-time position isn't going to help until you adjust your inner beliefs.

If you don't think you're beautiful, because you aren't thin, ripped, or pretty enough, then going to the gym every day, or having plastic surgery, isn't going to change that. Until you believe, in your soul, that you're gorgeous, you'll never see it.

How much money do you need to feel rich? The answer will vary from person to person. It isn't about a specific amount, it's about whether you believe you have abundance or not.

I've spoken with many people who set a specific amount of savings that they thought would make them feel safe. When they reached their goal, they moved the goalpost. Each time they saved their target amount, they realized it still wasn't enough. It was never going to be enough, until they released their limiting beliefs around finances.

1. Decide what you want to change in your life. Common choices are money, satisfaction, or relationships.

2. What do you believe about your chosen topic? You need to be brutally honest with yourself and delve a little deeper. Think about your parents' beliefs. It's likely they passed

limiting thoughts on to you without you realizing it. That's how so many subconscious attitudes get their beginnings.

3. Do these beliefs support the life you want? Tweak your existing beliefs or create new ones, so they align with the life you want to manifest.

4. Consciously look for evidence that supports your new beliefs. This often involves changing your initial perspective about your environment and circumstances. Paying a bill doesn't have to make you feel poor. Focus on the fact you have enough money to send your remittance and that you're helping someone else earn money.

5. Celebrate every step forward. Gratitude is one of the best ways to do this. Be grateful that you recognized your date wasn't a good fit before you got too far into a relationship.

You can't fake it till you make it in this work. Your brain is driven to support your true intentions, not the pretend ones. If you believe you will always have enough money, it doesn't matter if you have $10 in the bank or $10,000.

In a Nutshell

When it comes to psychology, it's all about what you believe, not what other people believe about you. How you perceive yourself is your reality.

Small-step Strategy

Changing the internal habits and beliefs of a lifetime isn't easy, but the payoff is limitless. If you want more money, believe you're already rich and deserve to be richer. If you want to be happier, see happiness in your current life and know more is available. If you want more love, start by loving yourself and believing you deserve to be loved.

EIGHT

Create a Mind Set for Happiness

Are you in competition, or in collaboration with the world? Do you try to be better than others, or do you work with them to create something more amazing than you could create by yourself?

Your answer to this question is probably linked to your mindset: those values and beliefs that affect how you view yourself and the world around you.

Do you believe that you were born with abilities and intelligence levels that never change, or do you believe that with work and dedication, you can get smarter and more skillful?

If you believe that natural ability is fixed from birth, you have a fixed mindset. If you believe that natural ability is the starting point, but you can grow your abilities and intelligence with effort and perseverance, you have a growth mindset.

It's easier to live a happy life if you develop a growth mindset because you accept that regardless of where you are now in your life, there's room for growth, improvement, and increased wisdom. You're more willing to take calculated risks, because you view failure as an opportunity to learn.

With a fixed mindset, you feel pressured to live up to the expectations of those around you, and the ones you place on yourself. You compare yourself to others to prove you're smarter or more talented than they are. You live your life in competition.

The fixed mindset sees the world in the context of winning and losing. Humans are programed to believe that winning is linked to survival, which it was in more primitive times. Put any human into a win-lose situation, and they'll do whatever it takes to come out on top. The outcome is all important. Not winning means you failed, and for someone with this mindset, failing means you are a failure.

Negative emotions assist you when you are in a win-lose situation; they give you a better chance to win. This is one of the reasons why people with a fixed mindset aren't as robustly happy as those with a growth mindset.

Many people with fixed mindsets think they have a growth one, because they consider that to be the "right" outcome. But living in denial won't serve anyone. You may discover that you have different mindsets in different situations. You might use one at work and a different one at home.

To help you make an honest evaluation, here are some examples. If you have a fixed mindset, you're more likely to:

- See life in terms of right and wrong.

- Have difficulty making decisions for fear of choosing the wrong one.

- Defend your intelligence and natural ability, and get upset if you think someone is suggesting you're wrong or not good enough.

- Be motivated to be better than other people and find reasons to justify why you are.

- Avoid taking risks if you aren't confident of success.

- Blame other people or things when you think you've failed.

- Be more interested in the outcome than the process.

- Give up if something doesn't come easily.

Breathe deeply and read the list again. This isn't about perfection, it's about awareness. Most people display a fixed mindset in some areas of their lives. Rarely are you all fixed, or all growth.

I was raised with a fixed mindset. It wasn't until I read *Mindset* by Carol Dweck that I realized there was another way to view the world. Since then, I've worked hard to develop a growth mindset. The best way to shift your viewpoint is to be aware of your fixed mindset thoughts and statements, and then reframe them into a growth mindset perspective.

FIXED: If I can't do it right the first time, I'm going to quit.
GROWTH: I'm not very good at that yet, but I want to get better, so I'll keep practicing.

FIXED: You didn't get a single A on your report card. What have you been doing at school?
GROWTH: How do you feel about your marks? Did you try your hardest? What can you do to improve? If you've done your best, then that's all you can do.

FIXED: We lost the game because the ref was useless. His calls always went against our team.
GROWTH: We did our best, but the other team was better on the day. Some of the calls didn't go our way, but that happens in games. Sometimes they go your way, and sometimes they don't.

FIXED: I hope he falls so I can win.
GROWTH: I want to win against the best.

As I mentioned, I was raised with a fixed mindset and have put a lot of time and energy into developing a growth one. I think I've done a pretty good job of shifting how I see the world, but I'm a work in progress.

Learning something new or participating in a group activity are times when I can suddenly find myself right back in its clutches. If the skill doesn't come easily, thoughts of giving up may swirl in my head. When working with others, if I'm not careful, I can fall into a trap of comparison.

When this happens, I find myself wishing I'd been raised with a growth view of the world. Starting with good habits is so much easier than having to break undesirable ones. Just when you think the old pattern has been buried, it crawls out of its grave to haunt you.

If you have young children at home, I urge you to work to develop a growth mindset. They learn by copying the significant adults in their life and you can give them a head start by gifting them with a mindset for happiness. Collaborating with the world will serve them better than competing with it.

In a Nutshell

With a growth mindset, you can concentrate on the journey you're taking through life, knowing you're the master of your own fate. You decide what you want and then put all your energy and resources into achieving it. You aren't trying to prove yourself to other people, nor do you feel you're in competition with them. There isn't any pressure to measure up to others, only a desire to improve and become better today than you were yesterday.

Small-step Strategy

Awareness is the first step to transformation and creating a connection to happiness. Your life provides you with opportunities to learn. This process is about growth, not perfection. Whatever your starting point, there's always more to discover about yourself and the way you view the world.

Read through the characteristics of a growth and fixed mindset. Be honest with yourself. There isn't a right or wrong perspective, just a way of seeing things that'll connect you more strongly with happiness. It's about choice.

NINE

Stop "Shoulding" Yourself

How many times a day do you use the word "should" or some variation of it? The best way to get an accurate answer is to ask a few people to be your "should police."

When I first started working with a coach, we talked about doing things because I felt they were important, not because they were expected of me. During our discussions, she would stop me every time "should" crept into my vocabulary. There were some very halting conversations in those first few months.

I've lived much of my life doing things that I felt were expected of me, even though I hated them. For example, when I lived in England, there was a regular social calendar of dinner parties to host and attend. Cooking is something I've never really liked or felt confident about. I do it to combat the sound of gurgling stomachs, not because it's enjoyable. I'm fine preparing meals for my family, but when other people are involved, I get really nervous.

Whenever I was hosting, I would spend a week or so experimenting with recipes. The day before the event involved cleaning the house, grocery shopping, and dreading what was looming. The day after involved cleaning the house, grocery shopping for food that wouldn't fit in the fridge because of the dinner party provisions, and relief that it was over – for a month or two.

In case you are thinking that, despite my worry, these dinner parties were probably a huge success, let me stop you right there. One time there wasn't enough food, and another time my guests enjoyed pie with a burnt topping. If you've ever watched the first Bridget Jones' Diary movie and seen the blue soup, you'll have an idea of what might be in your future if you came to my house for dinner.

Why did I do it? Because I thought I should. If you're invited to someone's house for a home-cooked meal, you should invite them back to your place to sample your culinary delights – even if you don't have any. If you get asked to help with an activity or event, you should say yes. If someone offers you a cookie to go with your coffee, you should take one.

When my daughter was ten weeks old, both my doctor and my midwife suggested it would be best for my unsettled baby to have bottle supplements. I agreed thankfully. She finally seemed to get enough to eat. But if I was in public, I would hide in a corner somewhere because I was ashamed. I should be able to produce enough milk to nourish my infant. Only bad mothers bottle fed their babies.

Can you relate to my story or any of my examples? Have you done things you didn't want to do because you thought you should? Are you still unconsciously letting that word have power in your life?

The time has come to stop "shoulding" yourself.

The best way to do that is to consciously discover who you are and accept that you are the perfect version of you for today. Don't hide your areas of challenge. Readily admit them, but work on growing and developing them. The best version of you probably looks nothing like the best version of your best friend, mother, or sibling.

I no longer consider my lack of culinary skills to be a weakness. I have lots of interests and talents, they just don't happen to be gastronomic ones. Today, when I entertain family and friends, I freely admit that there's no guarantee the food will be edible, or that I'll have made it myself. I doubt they care.

Once you know, accept, and love yourself fully, you can share your authentic self with the rest of the world. This is where confidence and freedom live. I like to be liked, but if I'm not, I can live with that.

In a Nutshell

You'll never reach perfection. There is no such thing. Concentrate on growing every day, not achieving a level you think you should be aiming for.

Small-step Strategy

Notice how many times you use the word "should" in your daily conversations. Get help from your family and friends if you need to. Awareness is the first step to transformation. In what areas of your life are you most likely to talk about things you should do?

Along with this awareness, begin to accept yourself as you are, without embarrassment or shame. Choose one way you're growing and do a weekly check to see how much.

TEN

Discover Your Zen

What do you want most for yourself and your family? If you're like the majority of people, your answer will likely be a variation on being happy.

We all yearn for this elusive emotion. It's elusive because we aren't designed to be happy all the time. That's why everyone has times when they think their life is horrible.

Your negative emotions are there to help you survive. Whenever your mind perceives you're in a win-lose scenario, your negative emotions help to focus you on your primary goal — survival. In primitive times, winning meant surviving and this programing is still with us today.

I believe living a happy life is achieved by being at peace with whatever's happening in your world.

Here are some signs that you're at war with your life:

- Do you get angry at little things, like when a driver cuts in front of you?

- Do you fume when you can't sleep because your partner is snoring too loudly, or if they chew too vigorously when they eat?

- Do feel tired and discouraged with life in general?

Being in a war zone is not ideal if you want a happiness connection. Finding peace is easier than you might think if you're aware of what's happening and are committed to making some changes.

Here are four ways to get started.

Stop Trying to Control Everything

I come from many generations of controllers. I'm not sure if it is in our DNA, or if we have just copied our elders. Either way, we are masters of overt and covert control. I speak from experience when I say, controllers live in humongous war zones.

No one will ever do things exactly the way you envision, so if you try to control everything other people do, you're bound to be disappointed and frustrated. People don't set out to upset you, it's just that they aren't you. They do things differently and have their own opinions.

It isn't just people that controllers want to fall under their spell. They have a false belief that things can also be controlled. If they behave in a certain way or follow a specific list of tasks, they'll get their work done or have a parcel arrive on time. Sadly, there are far too many variables involved in any action to ever be positive things will turn out the way you expect. This is one of the reasons you may think you made the wrong decision. Usually, wrong simply means you got an unexpected outcome.

I don't care who you are, the chance of you controlling the weather is slim to none, and yet how often do people melt into puddles of anger, frustration, and despair when it rains on the day of their big outside party? Learn to recognize the things you can't control and let them go. Be at peace with the outcome.

Be a Cheerleader Not a Director

This point is related to the one above. Everyone is on their own journey through life. Even your partner and children are taking their own treks. Share your wisdom and viewpoints, be there to cheer, comfort, and console, but let them choose their path and overcome their challenges.

Parents find this particularly difficult, but if your children don't learn to be responsible for their own lives, how will they manage when you're no longer there to make the decisions? All parents want their children to be happy, and regardless of what you believe, that won't happen if you're navigating their lives for them. They're not mini versions of you. They're individuals, with visions and lessons of their own.

Trust

Trusting yourself, and believing that whatever happens will serve you in some way, is key to finding peace. This is often easier said than done. It takes practice to trust you'll find a way through any challenge or to believe there's a gift in every situation, especially when it isn't easy to find.

Remind yourself of the difficult times you've weathered and all the ways they've made you stronger. Listen to your gut and believe in your ability to conquer whatever comes your way. You've done it before, so why should this time be any different?

Trust that your loved ones are learning from their own paths and will grow more by being in control of their decisions and accepting responsibility for them. If you encourage your children to make their own decisions when they are young, it'll be easier for them to trust themselves as they get older.

Everyone fails. Sometimes it's the best thing that could possibly happen. It's better to learn how to get up from a fall when you're young rather than waiting until you're in charge of a company.

Breathe

This may seem like a strange piece of advice, but when life is tough, you may find yourself forgetting to do this. Gritting your teeth, losing your temper, or holding your breath won't help you establish a sense of peace. Take a minute for a few deep, conscious breaths.

Happy people don't expect their lives to be constantly smooth or endlessly joyful. Instead, they work to discover their Zen so they can be at peace with what is.

In a Nutshell

Choose to trust that what happens in your life happens for you, not to you. There's always a lesson or opportunity to grow in every circumstance you encounter, both the good and the bad.

Small-step Strategy

Awareness is always the key to change, so start by carefully looking at your life. Are you at war with your situation or people within it? The next time you notice you're leaving your Zen zone, breathe deeply and then let go of trying to control the situation. Be curious about what gift the universe is bestowing on you.

ELEVEN

Be the CEO of Your Life

I have an irrational fear of falling. I can stand on the edge of a cliff and enjoy looking down – if I don't think I'm going to fall. But ask me to jump over a narrow stream and I need to summon courage. I might fall into that six-inch depth of trickling water.

The first time I went on a zipwire, I knew this fear was going to be challenged. I climbed up the tree trunk that led to the platform high among the branches. I allowed myself to be hooked into the equipment, and I waited for it to be my turn. I went to the edge of the wooden floor and sat down carefully with my legs dangling over the edge. I could have sat there looking down for hours, without a moment of nervousness. The distance to the ground didn't bother me at all. My issue was with the split second between sitting on the platform and starting my way down the wire. That moment when my brain questioned whether I would fall to the ground when I left the safety of where I was seated.

I looked down. My heart raced while my head told me to stop being so silly. I believe that I would eventually have worked up the courage to propel myself off the edge, but there were people waiting behind me and I could sense their impatience. I decided to take the easy way out. I looked up at the young man who was assisting each person.

"I think you are going to have to push me."

Without a moment's hesitation, he did as I asked. I was on my way through the trees before I had time to reconsider. It was exhilarating.

Everyone has fears. I've been speaking with a lot of people recently who are making major life decisions. Their fear of the unknown is palpable. What if it doesn't work out? Just like my zipline experience, mustering the courage to consciously plunge into the unknown is much more challenging than being pushed into it. If you get laid off from your job, you have no choice but to make a change. Deciding to leave because you want to work for yourself is much more challenging.

If your spouse finds someone new, you may be pushed into divorce. Choosing to leave because you want something more means that making the decision, and taking responsibility for it, are on your shoulders.

What if it doesn't work out?

What if I can't support myself?

What if I never find someone else to love me?

What if my new life is worse than my current one?

The number of "what if" questions you can create are endless.

How do you make a big decision when you have no guarantee that it will lead you to success or happiness? It might seem daunting, but it's also important to remember that choosing not to change doesn't come with a guarantee of success, either.

When I find myself faced with a choice that I'm nervous about, I approach it from two different angles.

What's the worst that can happen?

I don't look at this side to catastrophize and worry. I do it for clarity. In the case of my zipwire experience, I could have plummeted to the ground and been paralyzed or killed. What was the chance of that happening? Very unlikely. If the chance of something horrific happening was high, my decision to back out would have been an easy one.

If I wanted to leave my job, my worst-case scenario might be not getting another position where I made as much money. Is that something I could survive? I expect the answer would be yes, I could learn to live with less.

What good things might come as a result?

Let your mind dream big. Spend time visualizing the wonderful future that might lie ahead. Leaving your current work could make way for your dream job, or something totally different that you've never considered.

The last step is to weigh up the answers to both questions. Do the possibilities outweigh potential risks? Listen to your intuition and take time to decide. After examining both sides, I like to put it to the back of my mind for a while. Sleeping on it is more than just an expression. Often, when I wake up, I know what the right decision for me is. Some unknown part of my brain has worked it out for me.

Once you reach this point, try not to regret the past or worry about the future. Put your energy into making the present the best it can be. Live in the moment, not in the space of what might have been, or what could happen. Even if things don't work out the way you hoped they would, there are always lessons to learn and new decisions to be made.

In a Nutshell

It's important to be proactive in your life. Rather than waiting to be pushed into a decision or major change, take responsibility by making a conscious choice. Rarely do choices come with a set of guaranteed outcomes, but don't let that stop you. The only way to be empowered is to be the CEO of your own life.

Small-step Strategy

When you aren't sure what to do, examine possible outcomes for each of the choices. Ask yourself:

1. What's the worst thing that can happen?

2. What good things could come from making this choice?

Once you've done that for each option, compare your lists. If you still aren't sure, sleep on it and reconsider in the morning.

TWELVE

Allow Your Brain to Wander

I n my last home, I had an amazing shower. It was one of my favorite features in the entire house. I came to view it as a magic portal to clarity and creativity.

For many years, I wrote a column that was due in my editor's inbox by Saturday at 11 a.m. Whenever that day arrived and I still hadn't produced anything worthy of being emailed, I didn't panic. Instead, I got into the shower. I'd emerge from my steamy refuge inspired and ready to write.

Finding answers to problems or being struck by an "aha" moment when you're in the shower is by no means unique to me. Why does a good shower have such a powerful effect? There are a couple of reasons for this.

The human brain is an amazing organ, but it has its limitations. It can only give its attention to so many things at one time. That's why multitasking frequently results in more errors than if you focused on each task individually.

Doing multiple things at the same time means your brain is flipping its attention back and forth between tasks. Food can burn, a scheduled call could be missed, or the sink might overflow if your brain's attention is elsewhere at a critical time. Being overly busy makes it difficult for your brain to find time to discover the clarity or creativity you may be craving.

Another reason why you can shower your way to inspiration is that it allows your mind time to wander. When your brain relaxes, it opens up to new ideas and perspectives. Sometimes the thoughts you need aren't actually in your consciousness.

Your senses take in everything they encounter and send all that information to your brain. You'd be overwhelmed if you were made aware of all of that data. Your mind helps you by only sending information to your consciousness that it thinks will be helpful. That's why setting intentions can be so powerful. It lets your mind know what information you want your consciousness to receive.

Your brain sends data that it believes will support your values and beliefs, regardless of what they are. This is why you may know something but have no idea how. Information that's being stored in your subconscious isn't lost. It'll bubble up to the surface if your brain decides it'll be helpful to you.

Studies show that when you don't know the answer in a multiple-choice test, your best strategy is to go with your first instinct. Don't overthink it. Allow all of the information in your subconscious assist you.

What do you do if you run into a creative block or problem at a time when having a shower isn't possible? There are other things that will give you the same result.

Look for a solo activity that requires minimal attention. Take a walk someplace that doesn't require concentration; wash the floors; vacuum; or weed your flower bed. The trick is to disconnect from the outside world.

So, the next time you have a problem to solve or hit a creative roadblock, carve out some mental space by jumping in the shower or heading off on a walk by yourself. Allow your brain the time and space to provide you with an answer.

In a Nutshell

A great way to give your brain an opportunity to wander and discover a great solution or creative spark is to "sleep on it." Rather than pushing through and trying to make an answer come to you, revisit the situation after a restful night.

Small-step Strategy

Prepare yourself for using this method by choosing a solo activity that requires minimal attention. Have it in your personal growth toolbox so you can grab it whenever you need it.

Have you downloaded your 30 Affirmations and Reflection Prompts?

ReenRose.com/FreeResource

THIRTEEN

Be Empowered

I s life happening to you, or is life happening for you? There's an important distinction between these two phrases, although only one word has been changed. One leads you to believe you're helpless, while the other is empowering.

Thinking life happens to you is like seeing yourself as a pawn in a game where you have no control. Feeling happy or sad is forced on you by circumstance and the choices of others. With this belief, you're likely to spend time in victim energy. This is when you feel powerless to do anything to change how you feel about yourself or your life. It's as if people are doing things to deliberately hurt you.

Feeling victimized or powerless is common. You blame others, the world, or bad luck for your lot in life. How you feel isn't your fault. This may seem like an easy way to live because nothing's your responsibility. Other people make you mad, hurt your feelings, and do things to upset you. It may seem simple to relinquish accountability, but it's unlikely to provide long-term happiness.

If you were raised by someone who lived this way, you probably unconsciously developed this type of limiting belief.

Empowerment comes from understanding and knowing that your life belongs to you, and you always have choices. You're never a rudderless boat being battered by the relentless world around you.

When you believe life happens for you, you see everything that goes on in your world as a positive opportunity of some sort. It may be difficult to find the gift, but you believe it'll reveal itself at some point if you keep looking for it. Other people don't make you happy or unhappy. Sure, they can spark your emotions, but you get to decide whether to embrace those feelings or let them go and move forward.

You aren't here to direct anyone else's journey. See interactions as a dance with steps you may not know. What another person does or says is part of their pattern, not part of yours, although they may affect how you move. Stop blaming or taking credit for things that happen outside your own personal journey. Focus on your world, not on other people's.

Everything that touches you is for your benefit. That applies to the good, the bad, and the ugly.

Becoming suicidally depressed was a horrible time in my life, but without that experience, I doubt I would have realized just how important practicing happiness is.

I would have preferred my 30-year marriage to have made it to 50 years, but it didn't. I trust there's a purpose for that. I'm confident our decision to part ways was a good one for both of us.

If you want to increase your happiness, a good starting point is to examine your beliefs about the world and the power you hold. Find a perspective that empowers you, and trust that everything that's happening is serving you, and them, in some way. Work toward being your own hero or heroine. Only you can make yourself truly happy.

In a Nutshell

Learning and growing aren't always the easiest options. Uncovering old hurts and resentments are going to crack you open, but until you do that, you may struggle to step fully into your power. If the cuts are deep, work with a professional.

Rather than immediately reacting to events, pause and consider them. Trust that everything that happens serves you in some way, even if you can't immediately figure out what that is. Take responsibility for your actions and your emotions. No one is out there trying to make you miserable. They may be thinking about their own happiness, but more often than not, you aren't part of their choices or decisions.

Remember to focus on you, not the person or situation that's upsetting you. If you hold resentment, blame, or anger toward other people or circumstances, you have the opportunity to release those feelings and see your life in a whole new light. Someone may trigger your anger, but they aren't making you angry. You get to choose which feelings you want to surround yourself with.

Small-step Strategy

You don't need to understand why you feel the way you do. Choose the experience you want to have and release anything that doesn't support that. If you can't move on without a level of understanding, then as I said above, find someone to assist you.

FOURTEEN

Desire is Linked to Fear

Fear exists in everybody's life. There's a myriad of places it surfaces: commitment, rejection, and failure are but a few possibilities. It often disguises itself as a form of protection.

If you don't love deeply, maybe you can avoid being hurt. If you save as much money as possible, you'll be safe from whatever life throws at you. If you don't try anything new, you won't fail. Sound familiar?

However, if you avoid challenges and novel experiences, you run the risk of sinking into stagnation. A life ruled by fear often means never reaching your full potential or fulfilling your deepest dreams.

Here are a few ways fear may be showing up in your world.

Negative self-talk

Do you find the voice in your head planting seeds of doubt? There are many ways it can do this. It may be telling you you're not smart/creative/coordinated/thin enough to do whatever you're contemplating.

This is a form of self-sabotage, and is a common way for your mind to stop you from trying new things.

Blaming Others

Fear encourages you to blame outside influences rather than taking responsibility for your life.

Creating Stories

Like blame, excuses can be comforting when fear is ruling your life. The human brain doesn't like to have inconsistencies between beliefs and actions, so it makes up stories to explain why you don't push yourself into the unknown. Often, they support limiting beliefs that you carry with you.

Believing "Good Enough" is Good Enough

There's a subtle difference between choosing "good enough" because better isn't worth your time or energy, and being afraid of reaching for the stars in case you don't achieve them. Be aware of your motivation for believing "good enough" is good enough.

Fear is the flip side of desire. Are you scared of robbing a bank? Do you lose sleep over the thought of getting caught or shot in the process? Probably not. Why aren't you afraid? Because it's unlikely you have any yearning to rob a bank.

Desire is part of every human's experience. It lives deep within us all and can sometimes feel irrational and scary. When wanting something makes you feel uncomfortable, your brain may try to convince you to stop wanting it.

As with all personal growth, awareness is your first step to transformation. In order to move forward, you need to bring your fears out into the open and own them. Recognize that humans fear losing the things they desire most.

A fear of public speaking may stem from a desire to be heard or seen. A fear of commitment may be rooted in a desire for connection. Wanting to be secure may cause you to hang onto money and possessions rather than enjoying your resources.

The following suggestions can help you lessen your fears so you can achieve your desires.

Detach From the Outcome

Don't stop trying new things or meeting challenges because you're afraid they won't work out. Step into them, do your best, and then observe what happens without being emotionally attached to the outcome. Curiosity is your best friend.

Shift Your Belief

Believe that life happens *for* you, not *to* you. This attitude encourages empowerment rather than victim energy. The minute you think other people or situations are responsible for what's going on in your life, you're giving away your personal power.

Stop Making Excuses

The more you practice being accountable for your life, the better you'll become at overcoming your fears. Start telling yourself different stories around your worries. Start listening for the word "should" in your conversations. If you should be getting more exercise, why aren't you?

Banish Negative Self-talk

Words are powerful, especially the ones you say – or don't say – to yourself. Replace self-sabotaging talk with self-affirmations. Remember, if you tell yourself something often enough, you'll begin to believe it. Make sure your words are encouraging, loving and kind, not hurtful.

Adopt a Growth Mindset

Rather than seeing setbacks as failures, view them as learning opportunities. Finding ways that don't work can help you discover the one that does.

In the words of George Addair, "Everything you've ever wanted is sitting on the other side of fear."

In a Nutshell

Understanding the link between fear and desire can help you uncover what you want most. Once you've established that, you can set powerful intentions before courageously moving forward into the life of your dreams. It isn't always easy, but it's so very satisfying.

> ### Small-step Strategy
>
> Think of one thing you're afraid of. Is there a desire that's linked to that feeling? Don't rush this process. Take your time. Talk about it with a friend. Exploring is a valuable experience regardless of your conclusion at the end.

FIFTEEN

Take a Break

I can't count the number of times I've sat down to write and struggled. Sometimes I can't settle on an idea, or research is difficult to obtain. But there are times when I'm totally prepared with an idea and data, and I still can't get my words to flow or make sense. When this happens, I usually give up after an hour or two.

This used to bother me, and I'd worry I'd never be able to write easily again. With age and experience, I've discovered that this isn't the case. For the most part, when I sit down in front of my computer the next day, words and thoughts flow eagerly through my fingers.

It's a strange phenomenon, but taking a break can often be beneficial when you're trying to complete a task. This wisdom hasn't always been something I paid attention to. Not too many years ago, I'd force myself to power through a challenge rather than step away from it for a while. I thought I wouldn't be able to sleep if I didn't cross the troublesome task off my list.

It turns out the opposite is true. You may be sleeping, vegging, or daydreaming, but your brain is still busy. There's evidence to show that during quiet times, your brain reviews what it's learned or worked on and then ingrains it into your mind.

When I was learning to play tennis, a shot I struggled with during one lesson was suddenly possible the next time I stepped onto the court. Without realizing it, my mind had continued to work on the skill. It reviewed and processed without me even realizing it was happening.

This illustrates why I now tell myself and others to sleep on tough decisions, or to come back to a challenging task the next day. It's valuable advice that's helped me countless times over the years. Instead of refusing to stop, I now listen to my brain and my body. If they're telling me they're tired, I pay attention.

You don't have to wait until you've hit a wall before you give yourself a break. Psychologists have found that building regular pauses into your day has many benefits. These include improving your mood and performance. There's even some evidence that suggests morning breaks are more valuable than afternoon ones.

In a study from George Mason University in Fairfax, Virginia, university students were given a test that required them to monitor maps of railway lines on a screen. The task involved staying focused for the length of the exam. Half of the students were given a five-minute break halfway through. Then the subjects were randomly assigned an activity to perform.

They were asked to:

- Sit quietly

- Listen to music

- Watch a music video

- Choose between listening to music or watching a music video

- Do an activity of their choice, as long as they didn't leave the room

The results showed it didn't matter how they spent their five minutes, all the students in the break group performed better than the ones who hadn't been given this opportunity.

Taking a break can be a struggle for some people. There's a common belief that working through your lunch or powering through your day, regardless of how tired you are, means you'll get more done. This is unlikely to be true. Instead, you'll probably feel exhausted, frustrated, and actually get less accomplished.

The next time you feel your energy and concentration dip, try taking a different approach. Instead of hunkering down and pushing harder to get the job done, take a break. It doesn't have to be a long one, although optimum length, frequency and duration all vary from person to person.

Try doing something different to the task you're taking a pause from. If you're working alone, have a five-minute chat with a colleague. If it's a team project, sit quietly listening to music.

Taking a break from your taxes to work on somebody else's is unlikely to give you the rejuvenation you're looking for. It isn't enough of a change.

The human brain isn't designed to focus on one task for long periods of time, so maybe it's time to be more like a Kit Kat and have a break.

In a Nutshell

Taking a break is never a waste of time. Not only will it restore your energy in the short-term, but it can also help prevent burnout further down the road.

Small-step Strategy

Schedule breaks whenever you're required to concentrate on something for a prolonged period of time. Decide in advance when they'll happen and what you're going to do. The last step is to discipline yourself to take them. Make them non-negotiable.

SIXTEEN

Speak Nicely to Yourself

D o you believe you create your own reality? I've discussed this question with many people over the years and I don't want to go too far down that rabbit hole. I'm not suggesting you can necessarily create the circumstance your encounter, but you can absolutely affect how you see the world.

The perception you choose to embrace creates your reality. If you think the world is dangerous, then your world is full of danger. Another person, living in the same world, may believe it's a loving place and will find love around every corner.

This happens because of the way your brain works. You may hear with your ears and see with your eyes, but until your brain gets involved, there isn't any meaning attached. Your senses send raw data to the brain where it interprets them. Not only does it interpret the signals it receives, but it also decides how you should respond to it. It does this by using your beliefs, values, and past experiences. If you believe you need to lose weight, or that nobody likes you, that's what your brain will use to interpret what you see in the mirror or the expression on someone's face.

The uniqueness of each person means that your brain is likely to interpret things differently to anyone else. Much of this decoding happens subconsciously. Without conscious intervention, things you hear regularly, tell yourself over and over, or complain about become absorbed as truth.

I convinced myself that I had no hand-eye co-ordination, that I wasn't as smart as my siblings, and that I wasn't good enough - whatever that means. I also had the unshakable belief that I would get any job I interviewed for, that I was born to be a teacher, and that my life was blessed with luck. All these things, both the possibilities and the limitations, became part of my reality.

None of these beliefs were conscious choices. It wasn't until I learned about how the brain works that I realized letting my subconscious mind have unbridled control of how I interpreted the world wasn't my only option. I could choose to take a mindful approach and encourage my brain to interpret stimuli in a way that felt good to me.

This understanding is empowering. If you have the ability to choose how to interpret the signals your brain receives, why not connect to something that brings you happiness? A good way to release limiting beliefs and embrace new possibilities is through affirmations.

Affirmations are short, powerful statements that you repeat often. They can affirm good or bad beliefs. Negative self-talk is a type of affirmation. If you tell yourself over and over that people won't like you, that's how your brain will interpret the stimuli it receives.

Instead, start a habit of positive self-talk. Be deliberate and conscious of what you say to yourself. Create statements to support the things you want to be true. Repeating them daily can change your subconscious thoughts and beliefs and get your brain on the side of positivity and love. In other words, affirmations can help shape your perceived reality.

Use the affirmations provided in the free resource, or create one that's customized to your unique needs and desires.

What do You Want to Change, Support, or Create?

You may already know exactly what to choose. If not, free writing can be useful. Set aside a specific block of time to write down whatever comes into your head.

Don't think about it and don't judge, just write. When you're finished, read over your words to see if something jumps out at you. It might be a desire for something new or different, or a limitation you want to alter or release. Continue your sessions of free writing until you know what you want to accomplish with your affirmation.

You may have several things you want to affirm, but it's best to concentrate on one at a time. You want to give your subconscious mind time to absorb each affirmation as truth.

Create Your Affirmation Statement.

- Keep it short but powerful.

- Write in the first person. Rather than "love your life," say "I love my life."

- Write in the present tense as if you've already achieved what you want. Replace "I will get fit," with "I am fit."

- Keep it positive. Instead of saying, "I don't eat junk food," try, "I choose healthy food."

- Add emotion with words like love and gratitude. "I'm grateful for healthy food that energizes my body."

Repeat Your Affirmation Multiple Times a Day.

Create reminders in your phone or put them on post-it notes and leave them on your bathroom mirror, in your car, or beside your bed. Every time you see one of these notes, say your affirmation.

Try habit stacking. Repeat your affirmation when you finish brushing your teeth or washing your hands.

Change your affirmation as you notice your emotions behind it waning. You can stick with the same goal but state it in a different way. It's important to feel an emotional charge when you say your affirmation.

Don't worry about figuring out how you're going to turn your affirmation into reality. If you believe it's possible, your conscious and subconscious minds will help you find a way.

In a Nutshell

Each thought you have and word you speak are affirmations. Think of them as self-fulfilling prophecies. Are your comments encouraging a stronger connection with happiness, or are they strengthening a relationship with dissatisfaction and criticism?

Small-step Strategy

Speak to your deepest desires by creating affirmations that resonate with your soul. What do you want to create for your reality? If this is a new habit, begin with something small. Maybe you want to be healthier or feel more confident at work, but the sky's the limit.

Once you know what you want to strengthen, use the above steps to create an affirmation around it. Say it out loud and repeat it often.

SEVENTEEN

Become Your Own Spin Doctor

Remember the story of Rumpelstiltskin? He was a master of the spinning wheel, spinning straw into gold. Few of us use spinning wheels anymore, but you can still be a master, or doctor, of spin.

Mirriam-Webster defines a spin doctor as:

"A person responsible for ensuring that others interpret an event from a particular point of view."

Politicians rely heavily on spin doctors. You might not be running for public office, but you can become a happier person by becoming your own spin doctor. Be responsible for interpreting the things that happen in your life in a positive light rather than a negative one.

Getting laid off can be considered the worst thing that has ever happened, or as an opportunity to discover a new career path. You may not see the positive in a situation right away, but be confident that with the right mindset, one will appear – and it will. It's like having a door close, only to find a window opening.

Your brain is programed to find consistency between your thoughts and the world. It's uncomfortable believing a specific person is nasty and then watching them help a homeless person in a kind and caring way. Your brain wants the things it sees to be in line with the things it believes.

It works tirelessly to find evidence that supports your thoughts and feelings, and recalls and interprets information in such a way to confirm your opinions and beliefs. For example, if you think about how much you like your colleagues, you'll notice all the good things they do and interpret events with a positive spin. On the other hand, if you think you work with terrible people, the same events may be interpreted negatively, and your attention will be drawn to scenarios that show your colleagues in a negative light.

This fits with the law of attraction — what you think about is what you attract. Your brain does everything in its power to make sure this happens. I remember the first time I became aware of this. I was newly pregnant with my first child and walking through the center of Northampton in England. As I progressed down the street, I saw pregnant women and babies in prams – everywhere.

Had everyone suddenly become pregnant? Of course not! I just hadn't noticed them before because pregnancy wasn't something I was consciously thinking about. Once I became pregnant, my mind drew my attention to other women who were, or had recently been, in the same situation.

Strategies to Improve Your Spinning

- If you're unhappy with part of your life, like your job, or your marriage, try not to dwell on it. That isn't always easy, but focusing on negative things will encourage your brain to show you how correct your thinking is.

- You believe what you hear, even if it's your own voice that's doing the talking. Just like with your thoughts, your words will kick your brain into action to find evidence to support what you say. Use that fact to your advantage by talking in the most positive terms possible. If your words are positive, your brain will search for evidence to support that positivity.

- Put your energy and focus into sharing the good things that have happened to you rather than the bad ones. If you have to talk about negative experiences, try to add a humorous spin to the story, or mention a lesson you've learned as a result. You'll be amazed how talking about events in a positive light can alter a negative mood. The most embarrassing and outrageous situations make the best stories later.

- If you need to share something negative or sad, set a timer for five minutes. When your timer goes off, shift your words and thoughts to more positive topics.

- Stop negative thoughts when they first pop into your mind. Remember that your brain will endeavor to spin stories that support how you feel and ignore any evidence to the contrary. With practice, you can train your brain to automatically look on the bright side.

- Choose to remember good experiences and pass over the bad ones. You have control over what you think about and how you color your memories.

- Train yourself to think about periods of boredom or monotony as short-lived rather than long-lasting. Look for positive opportunities that they provide you with, like being able to listen to music, or if it's a physical activity, how it increases your fitness.

By adding spin doctor to your list of life skills, you can create a stronger connection to happiness.

In a Nutshell

Your brain's habit of spinning stories to support your thoughts and feelings is known as confirmation bias. When you know about its existence, you can work it to your advantage. By viewing your life in a positive light, your brain will find evidence to prove that belief is true.

Small-step Strategy

Choose one of the above strategies to add to your life. When you feel like it's become a habitual way of behaving, choose a new one. If you need a reminder, make some notes, and put them in strategic places.

EIGHTEEN

Manage Your Energy Efficiently

D o you have days when you feel worn out, anxious, or grumpy? I'm having one of those days as I write this. Strangely enough, I'm usually surprised when these moods arrive. Rather than a slow decline in my mood, it feels like a sudden shift. My life suddenly goes from happy to heavy. It leaves me wondering why I feel so drained and dissatisfied, when everything was going so well?

With few exceptions, this situation comes when I haven't managed my energy efficiently. Like when I'm in a creativity zone and don't want to stop in case I can't recapture the flow if I take a break, or when I've overcommitted to projects.

Everything you do, think, and create, takes energy. You probably know that, but do you have a management program to help prevent those heady highs from being followed by heavy lows? I understand the importance of having a plan to help me, but the fact that this situation keeps repeating itself shows that I'm not taking my own advice. I know when life is especially busy that I can't expect to stay as energized as normal without taking some special steps, and yet experience shows that's exactly what I think will happen.

Waiting until your battery is critically low, or has died completely, before recharging is not ideal. I'm confident that getting caught up in life and forgetting to check in to see how I'm doing isn't unique to me. With that belief in mind, let me share some thoughts on how to manage your energy.

Recharge

Your battery only works for so long before it needs recharging.
It's interesting how often people ignore this fact. You give and give and give and then you're surprised when you hit a brick wall; just getting out of bed seems like a challenge. At this point, it's easy to feel like life is getting the better of you. I find my mood takes a serious nosedive when I'm depleted.

Monitor Your Energy

Not all activities consume the same amount of energy. Getting caught up in drama and negativity takes more energy than being surrounded by peace.

Even facial expressions follow this tendency. Your muscles work harder to frown than they do to smile. Intense brain work or stepping out of your comfort zone will also zap your energy more quickly. Be aware of this when you plan your activities for the day, week, month, or year.

Make Energy Choices

Notice what's draining you and ask yourself if it's worth it. It's a little like shopping. Is that purchase worth the money? Just because something burns a lot of energy doesn't mean it isn't a good way to spend your time. Just make sure your choice is a conscious one.

You don't have to avoid high energy activities, but balance high energy work with energy replenishment. Don't be afraid to put things off. Deciding something isn't worth the energy now doesn't mean you can't come back to it later when your life slows down a little.

Monitor Your Energy

Don't wait until your battery is critically low before you start looking for your charger.

Be aware of how much energy you're using and what level your battery is at. When you're involved in high-energy activities, you'll need to recharge more often. If you are surprised at how quickly you're feeling depleted, examine what you've been doing.

Your Energy is Unique

Life would be simpler if you could recharge by plugging yourself into an outlet. Instead, you need to figure out what recharges your specific brand of energy. You may even discover that emotional, mental, and physical drains require different approaches.

Here are some common ways to replenish energy:

- Eating

- Meditating

- Taking a nap

- Spending time in nature

- Exercising

- Laughing

- Sitting in the sunshine

- Spending time by yourself

- Getting together with rejuvenating friends

- Gardening

- Reading

This is not an exhaustive list. Only you know the best ways to rejuvenate yourself.

Managing your energy is something few of us are taught at school or by our parents, and yet it's a vital skill. Start becoming aware of how you're feeling by checking in with yourself regularly during the day.

Ask:

- How am I feeling?
- Does my energy need a top up?
- Am I surprised at how drained I'm feeling?
- What has caused my loss of energy?
- Is what I'm doing worth it?

Monitoring and managing your energy will improve your quality of life exponentially by forging a stronger bond with happiness, evening out your mood, and fostering your joie de vivre.

In a Nutshell

Like so many things in life, your energy will ebb and flow. Trying to preserve it by not throwing yourself into hobbies, connections and work would lead to a very dull life. The secret isn't to keep it safe, but to replenish it regularly.

Small-step Strategy

Check in with yourself frequently to see where your energy is. If it's lower than you'd like, try one of my suggested strategies and then check to see if it's had the desired effect. What works for your partner or friend may not work for you.

There's a certain amount of trial and error involved in this process, but the effort will be worth it.

NINETEEN

Avoid Comparing Yourself to Others

When I first started teaching in England, I loved the idea of school uniforms. I'd seen how cruel students could be about the clothes their classmates wore and thought this was a much better system.

Of course, I was being naïve. It didn't take long for me to realize that people will always find something to compare. In the case of these prep school students, it was footwear, the cars their parents drove, and family holiday destinations.

Theodore Roosevelt called comparison "the thief of joy." I wouldn't argue with the sentiment of his words, but comparison is harder to avoid than you might think. It's a fundamental human impulse. As with many innate behaviors, it served an important purpose for our ancient ancestors. It was vital for primitive people to work together if they were going to survive. If one hunter was particularly good at tracking, then it made sense for him to lead the rest of the hunting party. He could then pass the baton to those who were better with their spears.

There are times in modern society when it still serves us to know who's got the best skills for a specific job. It's also helpful when the time comes to choose a career path. Being creative and good with words is important if you want to be an author. You need a benchmark to come to those conclusions.

Comparison can become a problem when it's not understood and managed. Used in the right way it can motivate you, but it can just as easily lead to feelings of deep dissatisfaction, guilt, remorse, and destructive behaviors like lying or eating disorders.

When you know comparison is challenging your happiness, you may decide to pretend you don't care what car the neighbors drive or how many times your sister goes to Mexico, but that isn't helpful, either. Emotions always surface at some point, in some way, often when you least expect or desire them.

So, if comparison is virtually impossible to avoid, how do you keep it from stealing your joy?

Opting out of social media can be helpful, but like with the students I used to teach, there's always someone and something you can compare yourself to. Removing yourself from platforms like TikTok or Facebook isn't going to save you completely.

People you identify closely with, like colleagues, neighbors family, and friends, are the ones you're most likely to use as a measuring stick. The areas you're likely to notice are the things you value like wealth, physical appearance, and relationships. From there it's a simple step to believing the grass is greener somewhere other than where you're standing.

Rather than attempting to purge yourself of this programing, I recommend you change your source of comparison. Take a look in the mirror. That's the person you should be thinking about. How do you measure up to the you of last week, last year, or even a decade or two ago?

If you can look in the mirror and know that you're doing better than all the versions of yourself that came before, congratulations. If you can't reach that conclusion, maybe it's time to make some changes.

In a Nutshell

You're programed to compare yourself to others, but this isn't a healthy habit if you want to be happy, especially if you judge yourself as not measuring up. Change your focus for comparison to yourself.

> ### Small-step Strategy
>
> Consciously notice improvements and growth in yourself. Are you a better version of yourself than you were previously? If so, you're moving towards happiness.

TWENTY

Balance Freedom with Control

I f you want to live a happy life, is it more important to have:

a) Freedom of choice?

b) Money?

If your brain is screaming, "The answer is b," then it's time to look at some research carried out at the Victoria University of Wellington in New Zealand.

Doctors Ronald Fischer and Diana Boer studied data taken from over 420,000 people from 63 countries spanning 40 years. They were primarily interested in discovering whether wealth or individualism (the opportunity to make your own decisions) was a greater predictor of happiness. Was the link between happiness and money stronger or weaker than the link between happiness and freedom of choice?

The doctors observed a very consistent and robust finding that individualism was a better predictor of happiness than money was. In other words, people who were given the opportunity to make choices and decisions for themselves consistently ranked their level of happiness higher than those people who didn't feel they had freedom of choice. Having, or not having, money did not necessarily reflect how happy a person was.

The research also showed that, for subjects who believed money was important to their happiness, that belief disappeared when it was compared to having freedom of choice in their lives. It seems that although money may be something you desire, you don't want it at the expense of free will.

Whenever I write about research that's looking at the link between money and happiness, I feel it is important to clarify an important exception. Research repeatedly shows that humans need enough money to meet their basic needs – to take it "off the table," so to speak – but once you reach that point, having more wealth doesn't make you significantly happier.

Having the ability to make choices in your life will increase your sense of well-being — as long as you don't have too much of it.

Do you feel you have too much or too little influence at work, in your relationship, or with your family? Both extremes have equally negative effects.

If you feel you're being micromanaged, or your voice isn't being considered, here are some tips to increase your level of choice, and decision making:

- If you have certain tasks that have been assigned to you, decide for yourself how and in what order you'll do them.

- Make decisions that you're happy with, rather than ones based on guilt and obligation. Tap into your intuition and gut reactions.

- Try a new skill or activity you have always wanted to explore.

- Set yourself a personal goal and work toward attaining it.

- Remember that you have the power to say no.

If you feel like everything's being left to you, here are some ways to help you decrease your level of choice and decision making:

- Ask for help.

- Involve other people by asking for opinions and advice before you make your decision.

- Find partners and team members to collaborate with.

- Let go of thinking other people won't do as good a job as you. Find opportunities to pass the decision making and task completion baton to someone else. Don't watch over these people or judge their process. Allow them to take responsibility for their actions and choices.

As with so many things in life, it may take time to find your sweet spot. It's only by experimenting that you'll find just the right blend of freedom and direction.

In a Nutshell

Not having autonomy or control over your life can cause you to feel unhappy, but so can having too much of either. Being micro-managed or being left without any guidance are both detrimental to your level of perceived happiness.

Small-step Strategy

Sometimes there's a fine line between happiness and too much or too little personal influence. Start with small changes as you test your "take charge" comfort zone. Be aware of how these shifts affect your mood. It's a little like being on a teeter-totter. You have to work to find the perfect balance.

TWENTY-ONE

Decisions Aren't Right or Wrong

When was the last time you had to make a really big decision such as:

- Should I change jobs?

- Is this the right person for me?

- Which house should I buy?

Decisions are part of life. Unless you let someone else take control of your world, they can't be avoided. How do you feel about making decisions, especially when they are major ones?

Recently, a friend told me he hated making wrong decisions. I was a little confused by his statement. How could he know he made the wrong decision unless he has a time machine and can go back for a do-over? The intriguing thing about a decision is that you only get one shot at making it. Even if you're faced with the exact same choice again, you aren't the same person, and your circumstances are different than they were the first time you chose. Imagining how an unchosen option might have turned out is just a guess, not a fact. You can never guarantee that any other choice would have worked out better than the one you made.

For example, let's say you have been offered two different jobs. After consideration, you make your choice. A few weeks into the new position, you discover it isn't the job you expected it to be, and you're convinced you should have taken the other one. How do you know the other job would have worked out any better? You may not have liked that one, either. Perhaps you need to look for a new career direction.

If you believe there are right and wrong decisions, the pressure of figuring out which is the correct choice may paralyze you into indecision. Not deciding is an option, but not one that happy people like to choose. Research shows that being in control of your life plays a major role in your sense of wellbeing.

Start by discarding the idea that decisions are right or wrong. Yes, there are foolish decisions made every day by millions of people, but sometimes the result of a poor choice is exactly what that person needed to get back on track. Some of the worst decisions lead to wonderful outcomes.

How do you break away from indecision paralysis?

- Rather than thinking your choices are right and wrong, see them as leading you on different paths. Either one could end up being amazing or challenging. Either way, you'll have opportunities to grow and learn.

- Don't let your mind project too far into the future when you're considering your choices. Think about it being for now, rather than forever. You can always change the direction you're going if you don't like where your decision is taking you. If you decide to work as a contractor because in 10 years, when you are ready to have children, you'll have more flexibility with your schedule, you aren't living in the present, which is where happiness resides. You have no idea what the world will look like in ten years. Perhaps working from home or setting your own work schedule will be the norm. Perhaps you'll change your mind and decide not to have children. Concentrate on what you want now, rather than worrying about a situation that may never materialize.

- Accept that a decision doesn't have to be perfect, it just needs to be made. Usually, it's a case of the positives outweighing the negatives, rather than one choice being all good and the other one all bad. Listen to your instincts. If you're drawn to one option, or repelled by another one, your subconscious is trying to talk to you.

The next time you have a major decision to make, keep these three thoughts in mind. Remind yourself that if you don't like the result of your decision, you can always make another one. Being able to course correct is a valuable skill.

In a Nutshell

Viewing decisions as being either right or wrong can limit your connection to happiness. They may not turn out the way you anticipated, but there's always a lesson to be learned if you look for it. You may even come to be thankful for what seemed like a bad choice, because it leads to something unexpectedly wonderful.

Small-step Strategy

Decision making is a learned skill that takes practice. Start with frequent small decisions to warm up your decision-making muscles. Then own the choices you make.

Some of my best stories start with the words, "Don't judge me. It seemed like a good idea at the time."

TWENTY-TWO

Seek Unconventional Beauty

What do you see when you look in a mirror? Do you appreciate the face that stares back at you, or do you find fault with it? How about when you look at your body? Do you immediately notice all the things you believe are less than perfect, or do you rejoice in what you see?

If you think these questions don't apply to you because you've removed all the mirrors in your home, or you refuse to look in them, you may be wrong. If you've chosen to ignore your looks, what's your motivation? Do you really not care what you look like, or are you afraid of the feelings that arise when you see your reflection?

I've struggled for most of my life with my body image. From the time I became aware there was an ideal body type, I knew mine was substandard. Sadly for me, teenage Twiggy was the epitome of the female form when I was at an impressionable age. My skeleton will never look like that. That's not to say I was overweight. But I was tall and slender with curves, not skinny and flat chested. I inherited my dad's large bone structure. It means I have a larger head, hands, and feet than the average woman. In my day, saying someone was big boned was a polite way of saying you were overweight. Even today when I look at pictures of myself beside other women, I distort what I see. It's hard for me to believe that I'm not the size of a barn.

I'm far from unique in my body shaming experience. Both men and women frequently struggle to see their beauty rather than their faults.

Recently, I came across a photo from my late 20s. I'm in a bikini, on a beach in Greece. I look amazing. That isn't, however, what I thought all those years ago. I didn't want anyone to take my picture because I knew it would look awful. But who listens to me? I'm glad they didn't. It's sad to look at that youthful image and know I didn't appreciate my shape. In fact, I actively disliked it. I still struggle to accept my body. My default behavior is to find flaws rather than to love myself without judgment.

Aging brings its own version of this madness. The media has encouraged us to believe that beauty is reserved for those who manage to continue to look young.

In an effort to help me with my struggles, the universe recently blessed me with an opportunity to see my beliefs mirrored in someone else. I spent some time with a gorgeous young woman who's struggling to see her natural beauty. She's doing everything she can to alter her facial appearance. Like me, she sees a distorted image of herself every time she looks in the mirror.

How can anyone believe they have to look like an airbrushed model to be beautiful? The idea seems crazy, and yet it's a common affliction.

Knowing something isn't the same as believing it in your soul. If you know you shouldn't judge yourself, but you still do, here are some ways to work towards a more peaceful and harmonious relationship with your physical self.

Abandon conventional ideas

Change the ways you define beauty. Rather than using traditional measurements, create new ones. Explore how the ideal body has altered through the ages.

Define beauty in ways that aren't physical

Your attitude and personal energy have a lot to do with your attractiveness. Practice letting your inner self shine through. That's where your true beauty lies.

Practice looking for beauty in real life

Stop looking in magazines and on social media for what you think is attractive. When you pass a person or meet up with them, consciously look for beautiful traits. It might be sparkling eyes, a ready smile, or lively energy.

Let your quirks and idiosyncrasies out into the open

Your authentic self is meant to be seen. You may find that you've hidden it so well that even you aren't sure who you are.

There's nothing wrong with wearing makeup or being fashionable, as long as you're doing it for you. If you don't want anyone to see your natural face, try ditching the makeup and dressing for yourself, not for others. If this seems scary, start slowly. Aim for a more natural look or start walking your dog before applying makeup. Your fear of being seen "au naturel" is likely to only be in your head.

Focus more on health than appearance

It's true when they say beauty starts on the inside. The glow that comes with a sense of wellbeing is better than any anti-aging cream you can buy. Mirrors and photographs rarely capture that.

It isn't your features that make you attractive, but the energy you carry. Reject the feature-altering filters on your camera and social media apps. This is like air brushing a photograph and re-enforces the idea that you should look differently than you do.

Practice happiness

If you're happy on the inside, it will seep through to the outside.

In a Nutshell

It may be difficult to change how society defines beauty, but you and I can shift how we do. I think Coco Chanel said it best.

"Beauty begins the moment you decide to be yourself."

Small-step Strategy

1. Choose one of the strategies laid out above.

2. Journal about your choice and the result it has on how you view yourself and your definition of beauty. This doesn't have to be done in one day. Check back every few days to start with. Success involves awareness and consistent action.

Twenty-three

Believe in Miracles

Do you believe in miracles? I do. I like the definition from the Longman Dictionary of Contemporary English. It defines a miracle as: "Something very lucky or very good that happens, which you did not expect to happen or did not think was possible." In other words, when unseen or unexpected possibility becomes reality, you have a miracle. Let me share a personal example.

When my dad developed a brain abscess in his 70s, we were told he wouldn't survive. It was possible, but the doctors felt it was very unlikely. He survived.

Then we were told he would never walk again. It was possible, but the doctors felt it was very unlikely. He learned to walk again.

The next limitation we were presented with was that he would never drive again. It was possible, but the doctors felt it was very unlikely. He passed his test and drove until he was 89.

All these feats were nothing short of miraculous, but they had a lot to do with my dad's attitude. He later said he saw my mom's face as she sat beside his hospital bed and knew he couldn't leave her. He made up his mind to do whatever it took to recover. He decided to embrace possibility rather than limitation.

Doctors, lawyers, and other knowledgeable specialists will tell you what they believe is the best information and advice. It's important to listen to them, but you get to choose whether to accept it or believe something else is possible. If you want more miracles in your life, don't limit yourself by closing your mind to what's possible, even if it isn't probable. Having faith when you're surrounded by sceptics isn't easy. It takes a lot of strength.

We need more miracles right now. That's why it's important to embrace possibility. If you think it can happen, it might. If you don't think it can happen, it probably won't. Few things in life are guaranteed. Even if the odds are in your favor, there's nothing to say you won't beat or be beaten by that one in a million chance. It's up to you to decide where you want to put your focus and energy. Do you want to dwell in possibility or limitation?

An exercise I'd encourage you to do if you are interested in this topic is write a possibilities list. Write down at least 100 things that you could have, do, or achieve if you wanted to. You might find this more challenging than you expected. I know I did.

Before I started, I thought I could whip off 100 things without pausing to breathe. The first 30 or so were easy, but then I began to slow down. My mind started to get in the way. I had to stop myself from thinking the only things I could put on the list were things I actually wanted to have or do and believed I had a chance of achieving. Instead, I reminded myself that money was irrelevant and just because I put it on my list, I wasn't committing myself to doing it. That made it easier to open my mind. I included owning a zoo even though I have no desire to purchase one, but should I change my mind, I could find a way to make it work.

The purpose of this exercise is to stretch your mind and expand your ability to find possibility in the most unlikely places. You don't want to limit yourself to what you've previously experienced, the amount of money you have in the bank, or what society tells you is possible.

Deliberately choose to embrace possibility, release limitation, and give thanks for every miracle you experience.

In a Nutshell

I believe in miracles because I believe anything that's possible can become reality. That doesn't mean every possibility will materialize, but I'm okay with that.

Small-step Strategy

Write a possibilities list. Try to include at least 100 things. Don't worry about how you could achieve them or where you'd get the money from. This is about expanding your mind into the unknown territory of possibility rather than what you think is realistic.

Twenty-four

Manage Feelings of Overwhelm

J ust when I thought I had everything under control...

Anyone who has sold a house, and isn't a Marie Kondo disciple, knows you can accumulate a lot of stuff in thirteen years. I made a plan that seemed achievable. I had booked a trip for just before the house was to go on the market, but I wasn't worried. I knew if I rolled up my sleeves and dove in, I could have the important work done in the five days between my return and my chosen date to list the house.

What I didn't expect was that I would pick up a bug.

I don't get sick often. I can't remember the last time I had a cold. I would have been happy with a cold. I could power through one of those. But this bug brought with it a flu-like chest problem that took me out at the knees.

I know I'm not the only one who has experienced illness or unfortunate circumstances striking at the worst possible moment. It happens to us all. I began to fantasize: If only this had happened a few weeks later, I would have treated myself to a few days on the couch, binge-watching Netflix. That idea sounded good in my head, but I realize it's unrealistic. Being sick is not like being on holiday. It's never fun. When you have your health, you truly do have everything. Perhaps I was overdue for a reminder of this fact.

It would have been easy to become overwhelmed by this situation. I'm pretty sure that would have been my go-to response a few years ago. I wanted to share my experience because I know this isn't unusual. Most people experience times when they feel they're in danger of drowning in their life.

Your unconscious response when things begin to pile up may be like mine. You may default to panic and catastrophizing. Just because you have a learned response, that doesn't mean you can't choose a different one. That's what I did. I chose not to be overwhelmed. Instead, I kept the following four pieces of advice top of mind.

You can only do what you can do

Get your thoughts away from what might be and back into the present moment. Worrying about what might happen if you don't get everything done isn't going to help you, and is likely to hinder. Negative emotions will push you into a fight/flight response. This isn't helpful if you need to find creative ways to solve your problems. It will contract your vision rather than expand it.

Don't suppress your feelings

It is okay to feel overwhelmed. Pretending you aren't stressed or unhappy takes a tremendous amount of energy. Acknowledging how you feel will allow those emotions to pass more quickly. Accept all your feelings, but don't let them slow you down.

Believe in yourself

You are designed to survive. If you get started, you will probably accomplish more than you expect. Prioritize and then look at individual steps, not the big picture. When I viewed what was happening in my basement, I chose to redefine the situation. Instead of seeing one big mess I created fifty small tasks.

Be kind to yourself

The older I get, the more powerful the word kindness becomes, and the more I strive to be friendly, generous, and considerate.

Too many people forget that this behavior shouldn't be reserved for others. You should also be kind to yourself. Don't berate yourself for not being able to find the perfect answer to a problem, or not getting your house decluttered quickly enough. If you need to take a short break, or promise yourself a treat when you finish, do it.

In a Nutshell

Being overwhelmed happens when you feel there's just too much happening for you to cope with. Some people are more easily overwhelmed than others. If you're like me and suffer from this affliction, take comfort in knowing this tendency means you get to practice your response more regularly. You can't choose what happens to you, but you can choose how to react.

Small-step Strategy

When life starts to get on top of you, breathe, remember that you are a survivor not a superhero, and be kind to yourself. When you start to feel more grounded, remind yourself of the steps outlined above.

TWENTY-FIVE

You Are a Work in Progress

"Don't air your dirty laundry in front of others."

"Never argue in front of the children."

"When a friend asks you how you are, say 'great' no matter how bad your life is."

I used to believe in these statements, but as time goes on, I agree with them less and less. Rather than portraying the image of a person who has it all together, I believe it's time we stood up and showed our authentic selves to the world.

This is especially true if you haven't got it all together. Why do I feel so strongly about the importance of showing the world your authentic self? Because I think it can help make the world a happier place.

You are a work in progress. There are always lessons to learn and new insights to gain. Your life is a never-ending opportunity to learn more about yourself and the world around you, but you are a perfect version of you – at this point in time.

You may nod in agreement with that statement, but do you really believe it's true? If you need a little clarity, here are a few questions to help you.

- Do you become frustrated when you can't do something right away?

- Do you want to hide your mistakes from others in case they think you're not good enough?

- Do you blame others when things go wrong?

- Are you hesitant to just be yourself in case people discover your flaws and shortcomings?

If you answer yes to some or all of these questions, there's a very good chance that you don't really see yourself as a work in progress. Instead, you believe you should be a finished product.

As a teacher, I've seen many examples of this mindset. Some students become upset because they don't know as much as others or aren't at the top of the class. The fact they're at school to learn, not to display that they already know everything, seems to have escaped them. If they didn't have anything to learn, why would they go to school?

When I was young and watched shows like *The Waltons* and *The Partridge Family*, I compared my family to their fictional ones and believed mine was abnormal. The Waltons and the Partridges didn't scream at each other, dream of being an only child, or argue over the chores.

Viewing yourself as a work in progress will boost your happiness. Rather than pretending your life is perfect, share your journey by showing the world your authenticity. It's comforting to know you're not alone. I might not have focused so much on my family's shortcomings if I'd realized our family dynamic wasn't unusual. We weren't perfect, but sprinkled among the less than perfect traits were many wonderful ones.

Happy people tend to be life-long learners. They're constantly gathering new knowledge, skills, and wisdom. That's an easier approach to take if you accept that you're a work in progress, not a finished masterpiece or a disaster. Spend your energy learning about and accepting yourself, rather than feigning perfection.

Pretending you're someone you aren't can be exhausting. Remembering what you want to hide from the world and keeping all the deceptions straight can be incredibly difficult. Take some weight off your shoulders and be proud of who you are.

Be open about the lessons you've learned and the ones you are in the process of integrating into your life. This will not only give you the opportunity to put your energy into positive growth and change, but it'll also allow others to see that they aren't the only ones who are a work in progress.

As long as you recognize your shortcomings and the areas that need some attention, it is okay to fall short of where you want to be. Awareness is the first step toward improvement, so start by becoming aware of the person you hope to become, and work towards that.

That doesn't mean you should stop striving to be the best version of yourself that's possible. Instead, accept that personal development takes time and won't necessarily be accomplished the first time you attempt a change.

In a Nutshell

You can help boost not only your connection with happiness but also that of the world around you by proudly being your authentic self, knowing that today's version of you is the right one for the journey you're on today.

Small-step Strategy

Take time at the end of each day to think about what you've learned and how you've grown. Set an intention for what you want to work on the next day.

Practice being comfortable with where you are now, knowing that it's possible to be an even better person tomorrow. Try creating an affirmation to help you.

*"I love the person I am today and will continue
to strive to be even better tomorrow."*

Me again.
I'm sure you know what I'm going to ask. Have you downloaded your 60 Affirmations and Reflection Prompts?

ReenRose.com/FreeResource

TWENTY-SIX

Take Responsibility for Happiness

Robustly happy people take responsibility for their own happiness. This is a powerful statement, and not one that I was ever introduced to by my parents. I don't blame them for withholding this vital lesson from me. My mom and dad didn't teach me this because they'd never been introduced to that principle, either.

It's not like I made a conscious decision to hand over the key to my happiness to someone else; I just copied what had been modeled for me.

Without really considering who should make me happy, I grew up thinking that happiness came from a loving partner, the circumstances of my life, and by doing my best to be a good person. That strategy may work for you; it worked for me for many years, but the happiness it provides is fragile. Remove your partner or other relationships, throw in some daunting challenges, and you may find your feelings of well-being slipping away.

Your parents are one of the most enduring examples you'll ever have. Similarly, you're one of the biggest influences your offspring will encounter. Children learn by observing and copying.

In the early years of life, you're likely to spend more time with your parents than anyone else, so you're bound to start copying some of their behaviors, beliefs, and values.

In the book *Secrets of the Millionaire Mind*, T. Harv Eker tells the story of a woman and a ham.

A woman bought a ham to cook for her family. When the time came to get it into the oven, she started cutting off the ends. Her husband was in the kitchen with her, observing her technique. Curious as to why she cut the ends off before cooking it, he questioned her. She thought about it for a minute, and then realized she didn't have an answer. She did it because her mom had always cut the ends off.

Intrigued, the woman decided to contact her mother. The resulting phone call was of no help. The woman's mother didn't know why she cut the ends off, either. She did it because that's what her mom had always done.

It wasn't until they talked to the woman's grandmother that the mystery was solved. The pan that grandma owned was too small for most of the hams she bought. The only way she could get them to fit was to cut off the ends. This tale illustrates just how powerful the behaviors of parents are. Each generation observed the action and copied it, even though they had no understanding of why.

It isn't just parents that act as models for others. The same goes for any adult who plays a major role in the life of a child, including grandparents and teachers.

And don't think you're safe if you don't spend time around the younger crowd. Adults copy the behaviors of other adults. That's why it's so important to think about the type of model you want to be.

Understanding this is empowering, but it's also a little scary. You're influencing the people around you whether you're aware of it or not, so make sure you model behaviors you're proud to know others are adopting.

In a Nutshell

Copying is a powerful way to learn new behaviors and skills. Whether you're conscious of it or not, you're both copying and modeling. Are you copying people you admire or just whoever happens to be around? Being more conscious of the behaviors you're absorbing and passing on can help strengthen your connection to happiness.

Small-step Strategy

Take time to ponder the following questions. Be honest with yourself. Use them as journal or reflection prompts or conversation starters.

- Are you modeling the beliefs, values, and behaviors that you want to see in the people around you?

- Are you leading by example and taking responsibility for your own happiness?

TWENTY-SEVEN

Smiling is a Super Power

I t's amazing how something as simple as smiling can boost your level of positive wellbeing. It not only makes you look more approachable, it can also make you feel better.

In fact, smiling offers a double whammy when it comes to improving how you feel. When your brain experiences positive emotions, it instructs the relevant muscles in your face to contract, causing you to smile. When a smile appears on your face, chemicals are released by the brain that make you feel even happier.

Smiling when I feel uncomfortable or frustrated is one of my go-to strategies. I've done this for many years, so you can imagine my delight when I discovered there is science to back up this strategy. It turns out that even a forced smile can make you feel happier.

Tara Kraft and Sarah Pressman conducted a smile study using chopsticks. Participants put chopsticks into their mouths to produce one of three different expressions: neutral, a standard smile or a big smile. Half the participants were asked to consciously smile while their mouths were forced into one of these expressions; the other half weren't given any instructions about smiling. Once the chopsticks were positioned in their mouth, each person was given activities to perform. These tasks were designed to increase stress levels. To see how each participant reacted to and recovered from the stress, their hearts were monitored. The results showed that those who were instructed to smile, regardless of what facial expression the chopsticks forced their mouth into, had lower heart rate levels and recovered from the stress more quickly, compared with those subjects who weren't asked to smile.

Those with chopsticks positioned to force a big smile had a slight advantage over less intense smiles, which suggests a forced smile can also reap the rewards that are associated with feeling happy. When comparing those people who were instructed to smile with those who weren't, the results showed that participants who had forced smiles from the chopsticks, but who hadn't been asked to smile, felt more confident and less stressed than those non-smiling subjects with neutral expressions.

It seems that smiling, regardless of whether it is genuine or not, tricks your brain into thinking you are happy. Additional research into this chicken-and-egg situation shows that when your brain feels good, it tells you to smile, and when you smile, your brain feels good.

One British research scientist declared that "smiling can be as stimulating as receiving up to 16,000 pounds sterling in cash." With the current exchange rate, that's between $30,000 and $43,000, depending on which side of the 49th parallel you live.

After reading about these studies, I decided to test their findings for myself. I waited for a moment in my life when I was feeling a slump in positivity. I arranged my face into the biggest, most genuine smile I could muster, and guess what? It worked. I could feel tension roll away from my neck and my whole body began to relax.

The next time you're feeling stressed, choose to turn your frown upside down. Your brain, your body, and your mood will thank you for it.

In a Nutshell

It may seem too simple to work, but research shows that smiling will make you feel better, even if it's fake. This is a super power you should cultivate if you want a stronger happiness connection.

Small-step Strategy

Notice how much you smile and look for more opportunities to put a grin on your face.

If you aren't good at smiling, or it makes you feel uncomfortable, stand in front of a mirror and practice. Try to make your smile reach your eyes, not just change your mouth; visualize yourself talking to someone who makes you smile or try remembering a happy experience. The more you practice smiling, the more comfortable you'll feel doing it and the more natural it'll feel.

If you notice your mood dipping, force a smile. The bigger the better.

TWENTY-EIGHT

Be Curious

D id you know that having a strong sense of curiosity is considered a sign of good mental health? When humans are born, they're naturally inquisitive. You just have to watch young children for a while to see the truth of that statement.

Swiss psychologist Dr. Jean Piaget defined curiosity as the urge to explain the unexpected. This impulse to find out more aids learning and development. Sadly, many people lose this natural curiosity as they age. Why? Research links the awareness of others evaluating you with the decline of inquisitiveness.

Children enter school as thirsty sponges ready to absorb new information, until they realize they're being compared to other children and then graded for their performance. Suddenly it becomes more important to achieve the goals the teacher sets out than to figure out how many ways you can make noises with your chair. Schools also tend to focus on finding the "right" answer rather than exploring possible answers. That approach discourages creativity.

Not that many decades ago, it was believed brains developed and grew until a certain age, and then their cells slowly started to die off. It was thought that as you aged, you became less able to learn new things. More recent research is disproving that theory. Scientists are finding the older human brain has a much greater capacity for learning and development than previously thought possible. The study of neuroplasticity shows the pathways in your brain can develop and strengthen, even when you're older. Your brain is a muscle and the more you use it, the stronger it gets. Likewise, if you don't exercise it, it'll get weaker.

There's no reason for your curiosity to die as you grow older, but it does. You may have stopped learning or striving for new goals, choosing instead to rest on your laurels and enjoy what you've already achieved. If you think your level of curiosity could use a boost, here are just a few ways that can help you spark it back into life.

Ask questions

This can occasionally feel like a dangerous thing to do, but it isn't. The only way to take a conversation to a deeper level is by asking questions. Ask and listen with an open mind full of curiosity rather than judge the responses.

Explore somewhere new

This can be a new holiday destination, but it can just as easily be a local restaurant or neighborhood park that you've never visited. New environments are full of opportunities to encourage a curious mind.

Do something unexpected

When was the last time you did something new or different? If it was last week, congratulations. If you can't remember, it's time to change that. Getting started is easier than you may think. Take a different route on your daily walk, or go to a different grocery store where you have to hunt for the items you need.

Learn about something new

This can be as simple as Googling a player on your favourite hockey team to find out more, or can involve randomly choosing a person, place or thing and seeing what you can discover.

Revisit childhood pastimes

What did you love to do when you were a child? Maybe you loved to color, you'd spend hours on a swing, or you liked to go skating. How does it feel to do the same activities at your current age? This is a great topic to journal about or share with a friend.

Be careful to observe rather than judge. This isn't about discovering talent or being the best. It's simply an opportunity to hone your learning skills.

In a Nutshell

Happy people are life-long learners. Learning comes when you allow yourself to be curious. It doesn't matter how old you are, it's never too late to rediscover your inquisitive nature. Doing this will strengthen your connection with happiness.

Small-step Strategy

Do one of the activities listed above. Journal about your experience. Record your thoughts before you begin and again when you've finished.

These prompts can help you.

- What activity did you choose?

- Why did you choose this one?

- Describe your feelings and emotions as you get ready to start.

- Did things go the way you'd planned?

- How do you feel now you're finished?

- What did you learn? Think about yourself, the activity, or anything else you observed.

TWENTY-NINE

Nurture Resilience

I experienced a situation in my 20s that left me forever changed. I wasn't physically different, but I was mentally and emotionally stronger.

When I was on my teaching exchange year in England, I decided that one place I had to visit was Egypt. I couldn't find anyone to come with me, so I signed up to take a ten-day tour. I thought I'd be on a bus with dozens of other people. That alone would be a challenging new experience. I hadn't traveled much on my own and I hadn't visited many foreign countries. I flew from London to Cairo and was greeted at the airport and transported to the hotel. I had a few hours before the orientation meeting, so I wandered the luxurious lobby with its glittering shops.

That is when I first realized I was going to be in for some unwanted attention. I looked younger than I was, and my blond hair stood out. I assured myself that everything would be fine as soon as I met up with the other people I'd be traveling with.

You can imagine my horror when I went to the orientation and discovered I was the only one on my tour. There was another tour with two couples on it. We spent the first two days together before they started their Nile River cruise, and I took a train to Luxor.

This was before the internet or cellphones were common, so I couldn't even share my concerns with anyone. I wanted to go home but couldn't afford to buy another ticket.

In truth, I also didn't want to miss out on the opportunity to see the pyramids, the Valley of the Kings and all the other places I was so fascinated by. My only option was to make the best of a situation that sucked – big time.

I was scared to leave my room, but I got hungry, and food was included in my package. Once in the dining room, I wanted to sit in a corner by myself, but instead was surrounded by the all-male wait staff. Any time I stepped out of my room, I was the center of attention. I dreaded it, but not enough to stay in there and hide.

The tours I had signed up for while I was in England were solo affairs. I'd get picked up by a taxi, dropped at the appropriate venue, and then retrieved and transported back to the hotel. I'm not sure I'd ever been in a taxi before, so I'd have been nervous taking one by myself in Canada or England, much less in Egypt.

On my last morning in Luxor, I decided to go to the open-air market. I asked for directions at the front desk and was told that walking wasn't very safe. They suggested I take one of the horse-drawn carriages that were on the street outside.

This sounded like a good idea, until the man driving it decided we should go to an undisclosed place to smoke hashish. I had to threaten to jump from the moving vehicle for him to take my choice of destination seriously.

Every night when I arrived safely back in my room, I congratulated myself for standing up to the challenge and counted the number of sleeps until I got home. I was in a relationship back in Canada, and I desperately wanted him to be with me. For the first six or seven nights, I mourned that he wasn't.

On about the seventh night, I had a sudden life-changing realization: I didn't need someone to save me. I was doing just fine on my own. Having company would have been a bonus, but I didn't need it. I also realized that if I could survive this experience, I could survive anything.

This challenge gave me evidence that I am a resilient survivor. I went from knowing that in my head, to believing it in my soul. I had forged a connection with my inner strength and happiness.

I've spoken and written about this experience many times because it forever changed me. It presented me with evidence of my resilience. It taught me that I can do anything – if I need to. I don't need to be in a relationship or to have help from another person to survive. Those things are good, but not vital. I can survive all on my own.

It takes a special person to enter the scary world of challenge, especially if it's a place you haven't spent much time in. Challenges provide opportunities to learn, grow, and change. They help you grow in mental strength and confidence.

So, the next time you're confronted by one, smile, roll up your sleeves, and show yourself just what a survivor you are.

In a Nutshell

Survival is your number one drive.

Often, the challenges that lead you to big changes are the ones you wouldn't choose for yourself. Instead, you're forced into them. I would never have chosen my Egypt experience, but I'm glad it chose me.

Small-step Strategy

Think about a time when you were faced with a huge challenge and lived to tell the tale. What strategies did you use to survive? This is a good subject to journal about. If you write your experience down, you can use it as a reminder of your ability to survive the next time you encounter a tricky situation.

THIRTY

Change is Good for You

Change is something humans are programed to dislike and yet, try as you might, you can't avoid it. You might think your life is the same, but there are always subtle shifts occurring.

"You can never step into the same river twice."

Heraclitus

The first time I encountered this quote, I had to read it a couple of times before I understood its meaning. By the time you step back into the river a second time, it's shifted. It isn't exactly the same as the first time you entered it.

Just like when a parent tells their child to eat their vegetables because they are good for them, change is good for you.

Change forces you to learn

Your brain is designed to learn. Humans feel happy when they master a new skill or gain a fresh understanding. Despite this, not everyone chooses to keep learning. When life changes, you have no choice but to change with it.

Change proves you can adapt and be resilient

Humans are amazingly adaptable and resilient. This means you can recover relatively quickly from the challenges that come along with change. You may know you're resilient, but it isn't until you prove it to yourself through experience that you really believe it.

Change forces you to leave your comfort zone

The greatest opportunity to discover your resilience is when you step into the unknown. You may do this regularly, but many people struggle to leave what they know and feel comfortable with.

Change presents you with new opportunities

As your environment changes, you'll find yourself presented with new opportunities. The key to taking advantage of these things is to be open to accepting them and discovering what they have to teach you. New isn't bad, it's just different.

Change keeps your life from becoming stagnant

Humans need a level of certainty to feel safe, but they also need newness and uncertainty. Without it, you'll probably feel bored with your life. Whether you choose to seek it or not, change will make sure you experience the mystery and surprises that life has to offer.

Change encourages you to examine your values and beliefs

What values are most important to you? What do you believe about the world you live in? Knowing the answers to these questions provides invaluable insight into your daily life.

One of my top values is autonomy, or the freedom to decide how I perform my work and live my life. When I became aware of the importance of this personal value, I suddenly understood why working for a micromanaging boss drove me to distraction.

Don't assume that these values and beliefs will never change. Experiencing major shifts is the perfect time to re-evaluate. You will either reaffirm they are still the same, or you'll discover both you and your beliefs have shifted. This information is invaluable.

Change makes you more compassionate

It only takes a few months of waiting tables to give you a whole new perspective on tipping.

Experiencing mental illness, or watching a loved one struggle, leaves you with an entirely different level of compassion for others who live in its grip.

Being jolted into a new situation you didn't ask for and don't welcome gives you a closer relationship with your emotions. This can provide you with a greater level of compassion for yourself and your fellow humans.

Sometimes the shifts are gradual, but they can also be abrupt. The unexpected death of a close friend or family member, sudden loss of a job, or a natural disaster are the types of change that you notice most. But if you're paying attention to your life, you'll notice many little changes too. Both types are equally important and will give you an opportunity to see just how resilient you are.

In a Nutshell

You may feel uncomfortable when your world gets rocked, but console yourself with the knowledge that change is good for you. It's your choice as to whether you view the new events as bringing possibility or limitations.

Small-step Strategy

Brainstorm reasons why change is good for you. If you struggle with this, enlist help from friends. It's easier to come up with creative ideas when you're with others. Don't stop until you have at least three explanations that resonate.

Remind yourself of these benefits whenever you notice yourself groaning about something not staying the same.

THIRTY-ONE

Puzzle Your Way to Happiness

How many of the gifts that you received in December of last year do you remember without having to pause and think? If you struggle to think of any, you're not alone. Unless there's a reason for it to stay at the forefront of your memories, out of sight really can mean out of mind.

This year, one particular present bucked that trend in my world. I received a murder mystery jigsaw puzzle from my sweetheart. As soon as I opened it, memories of spending time with my mom washed over me. Not because of the subject, but because of the activity. When I used to go back to my parents' house for visits, my mom often had a jigsaw spread out on the dining table. We'd spend hours chatting as we tried to complete the complex picture.

I hadn't indulged in this specific activity in years, but when I excitedly opened the box and got started, I was hooked. On my next visit to Costco, I saw a display of jigsaws and bought myself another one. My collection has now grown to almost a dozen. I've been averaging about a puzzle a week. Sometimes I only spend a few minutes during the day, other times I may be there for an hour or two. The 1000-piece puzzles seem to be my sweet spot. They're challenging yet not overwhelming.

I love the time I spend on this activity, but it's brought with it some unwelcome thoughts. They mostly revolve around time-wasting. Shouldn't I be doing something more productive?

Whenever I voice these concerns to my partner, he shuts them down by pointing out that it's important to quiet my often overly busy brain and have time to simply be. It's hard to argue with his perspective, but I needed more. Is there any other benefit to this activity?

It's well documented that Sudoku, crosswords, word searches, etc. can help keep your brain healthy and active. But what about jigsaws? I went on a hunt to see what science had to say about this specific type of puzzle. It turns out that jigsaw puzzling goes beyond entertainment. It helps cognitive, physical, psychological, neurological, and social skills.

Cognitive

This has to do with the processes of the brain; it includes memory, problem-solving, and the ability to concentrate. When you work on a jigsaw, you formulate theories and then use trial-and-error to test them. This process can significantly improve problem-solving and critical thinking, not to mention short-term memory and virtual-spatial reasoning.

The typical human brain has two sides. The left is responsible for logic while the right takes care of creativity and intuition. In order to complete a jigsaw or other puzzle, you have to engage both sides of the brain. This enhances cognitive functions like productivity, attention to detail, and mental agility, as the two sides are required to connect and communicate.

Physical
Moving pieces is good for fine motor skills and improves manual dexterity. This is especially important for the very young or elderly.

Psychological
This is the area my partner immediately identified as beneficial for me as it relates to the human mind and feelings. Spending time with a jigsaw puzzle helps reduce stress and anxiety. It quiets the mind by distracting you and providing you with an opportunity to enter an almost meditative state. Studies have found that spending just thirty minutes a day for eight weeks working on jigsaw puzzles can significantly reduce anxiety levels.

They also discovered that jigsaw puzzling can increase your feelings of happiness and satisfaction. The act of finding pieces that fit together releases dopamine. This is the neurotransmitter that's responsible for regulating mood and increasing optimism. The more successful you are, the more you want to continue so you can get even more dopamine.

Neurological
Your nervous system, or the signals between your brain and the rest of your body, is probably the area of benefit that gets the most attention when it comes to doing puzzles of any sort. Research shows that working on puzzles, including jigsaws, may actually delay Alzheimer's and dementia.

This is because the activity promotes neuroplasticity, or the ability to make new pathways in the brain when old ones have been damaged or pruned from lack of use. This process may happen more easily when you're young, but it occurs regardless of your age, as long as you encourage it. Jigsaw puzzles are the perfect activity to help you create new neural pathways and keep your brain functioning well.

Social

Working together on a jigsaw can be a rewarding social activity. It fosters collaboration and a sense of achievement. It was a strategy I used when I taught elementary school. I always had a puzzle table where students could go when they'd finished their work.

So, it seems that my new hobby isn't a waste of time. In fact, I'm doing myself a favour every time I settle down to find the right place for a few more pieces.

In a Nutshell

If you haven't completed a jigsaw puzzle for a while, or ever, I encourage you to give it a try. You may be surprised at how much you enjoy it. And if your brain suggests you're wasting your time, enlighten it by sharing all the ways you're helping both it and the rest of your body to be happier and healthier.

Small-step Strategy

If you want more family time, try my mom's strategy, and start a puzzle. Invite everyone to participate, but don't apply any pressure. You may be surprised at the results. There's something alluring about joining in on the quest to complete the picture.

THIRTY-TWO

Know Yourself

Can you remember a time when you or someone else broke an ornament or some pottery that you really loved?

One Christmas, I knocked a piece of my German village off the shelf in my front hall. As I bent down to retrieve it, I said a little prayer for it to be in one piece. That wasn't the case. I sighed and reminded myself that it was only an object.

It wouldn't be easy to replace, because I'd collected it and the rest of the village when I visited a Christmas market in Hamburg. I consoled myself with a reminder that I still had the rest of the village. It was okay that there wouldn't be a gluhwein stand anymore. But then I looked at the pieces in my hand. They weren't tiny shards. Maybe I could glue the heads and other separated parts back on. If I was careful enough, I might even be able to hide the fact that it had fallen at all.

This reminds me of the attitude many people, including myself, have towards life: Things happen. We get scars, bruises, breaks, and wrinkles. How do we deal with them? We try to patch them, so they don't show. The same thing happens to mental and emotional wounds. We try to bury them and pretend they aren't there.

Perfection is celebrated in all sorts of ways in our society. In the world of antiques and collectables, the closer something is to being in perfect condition, the more it's worth. At school, we value top marks over effort and learning, even though research shows that how well you do in school doesn't predict the success you'll have in life. Wrinkles, scars, and physical deformities tend to be viewed with sighs and sadness. We want to be perfect. Aging is fine, as long as we don't look like we've aged.

Society teaches you to try to piece yourself back together well enough that the resulting scars are camouflaged. The goal is to look unchanged, unless of course you judge the change to be a positive one.

Perhaps instead of modeling our personal repairing techniques on the perfection model, we should be following the Japanese art of Kintsugi.

Kintsugi is a technique used to fix broken pottery. Instead of trying to hide the cracks and flaws, it highlights them. Pieces are joined with a special tree sap mixed with powdered gold, silver, or platinum. The fractures are emphasized and made beautiful instead of being hidden.

What was once broken, and could easily have been discarded, is given a second life. The resulting piece is often more valuable than before it was damaged.

To embrace this philosophy, you may need to uncover the person at the center of the camouflage and repairs.

Aristotle said, "Knowing yourself is the beginning of all wisdom."

I believe that it is also the beginning of confidence, resilience, strong connections, happiness, success, and health.

In a Nutshell

"What is normal for the spider, is chaos for the fly."

Morticia Adams

I love this quote because it illustrates that it's possible for individual people or creatures to have a different perspective of the same situation. Creating a web to catch insects serves the spider but isn't so advantageous for a fly. Imperfection can be viewed in the same way. You can see cracks as something undesirable, or the beauty of survival.

Small-step Strategy

Consider the following prompts. If you keep a journal, write down your thoughts around each one.

- Imagine how different life would be if everyone stopped trying to be perfect.

- What does perfect even mean?

- Who decides what perfect is?

THIRTY-THREE

Find Peace in Exhaustion

D o you experience periods of exhaustion? I'm sure it's something most people can relate to. How do you deal with it? If you're like me, you may choose to gift yourself with some self-care and yet discover that, after spending a week recuperating, you're still so very tired.

It might seem like one tough day causes exhaustion, but it's more likely to be one difficult day on top of pressures that have been going on for weeks, months, or sometimes even years. If it takes that long to deplete your energy, why would you expect to replenish it in a fraction of that time? It's like taking an hour to walk somewhere, and then believing you can travel back on foot in five minutes. Energy doesn't flood in and seep out; it moves in both directions at the same rate.

If you've mismanaged your energy and have reached near collapse, here are five things I encourage you to focus on.

Accept what is

Rather than pretending everything is fine and continuing to push through your tiredness and lack of motivation, accept the reality of your situation. Be realistic about what's going on. Sometimes acknowledging the truth of what's happening can provide some welcome mental relief.

Take as much time as you need to recover

Just because you earmark a specific length of time to focus on recuperating, that doesn't mean you'll be completely recovered when it ends.

It's okay to feel tired. It's okay to need more time. Don't put pressure on yourself for it to be different. This is especially true if you're still caught up in a situation that's draining your energy. Recovery will take as long as it takes. Setting an end date is unrealistic and unhelpful.

Choose a healthy lifestyle

Eat well, drink lots of water, get plenty of sleep, exercise, and try not to add unnecessary stress to your life. Be okay saying no when others ask for help. Prioritize yourself.

Pay attention to how you feel

When a feeling of tiredness washes over you in the middle of the afternoon, try to rest or take a nap. If something feels stressful or hard, leave it until it feels less challenging. This isn't always possible, but even skipping a few tasks can make a difference.

Minimize Pressure

If you love making to-do lists, skip them for a while. You can still be aware of what you want to accomplish, but don't push yourself with specific timelines. Let taking a small step in the right direction be enough until you feel stronger.

In a Nutshell

Life isn't a race. There's no link between the speed of your recovery and how good or competent a person you are. There are no extra marks for how quickly you bounce back from physical, mental, or emotional exhaustion.

Find peace in exhaustion by listening to your body, accepting your situation, and finding moments to enjoy your life.

Small-step Strategy

When you notice your energy has been depleted, make a recovery plan. Here are some ways to get started.

Three things I can do to be healthier are:

Every time I _____, I'm going to consciously take 3 deep breaths.

Even though I'm feeling exhausted, I'm grateful for:

Pause and check in with yourself regularly through the day. Set an alarm if necessary. Ask yourself how you're feeling. What can you do to improve your energy right now?

THIRTY-FOUR

Self-awareness is an Asset

Having been invited for a family dinner on Easter Sunday, I decided to buy tulips for a hostess gift. My partner suggested I also buy some for our house. I chose three different colors, thinking we could give two bunches away and have the other one for ourselves. My partner thought combining all three colors would be better. He created a bunch to take with us and left the rest to be arranged later.

The next day, I went for a walk while he went to visit with his mom. I hadn't given the flowers much thought, but when I got home, I noticed they'd disappeared. I knew my partner wanted to give some to his mom, but surely not all of them? That didn't seem fair. Didn't I deserve some cheery blooms, too? In a very short time, I went from feeling happy to a state of agitation.

This may seem like a silly story, but often it's the little things that trigger you and send you into a negative spin. Frequently this happens because your brain gathers information and then jumps to a conclusion that may or may not be true.

As is often the case with your brain, this behavior has evolutionary origins. In primitive times, taking too long to identify threats could end your life. Today, this outdated programing can lead to incorrect conclusions and poor decision-making.

This is where self-awareness becomes an asset. When I noticed my negative emotions, I wondered whether they might be the result of an incorrect conclusion. This awareness is all you need to slow or stop the spin.

So, what do you do if you think you may have joined the dots incorrectly? Here are a few strategies.

Pause

Slow down your brain to avoid making a snap decision.

I took a couple of deep breaths.

Observe

Actively look for information that disproves your initial conclusion.

I looked around the house in case they'd been placed in a different room. There was no sign of them.

Think

Consider other possible explanations.

I reminded myself that just because I couldn't see them didn't mean they were gone. I couldn't think of another scenario, but I was willing to accept there might be one.

Question

Ask yourself whether your conclusion fits with what you know about the person or people involved in the situation.

My partner isn't naturally thoughtless or uncaring. I knew if he'd taken all the flowers to his mom, he must have felt she needed them more than we did.

Avoid overreacting

Keep things in perspective.

I reminded myself that I was getting annoyed about something that didn't deserve that much of my focus and energy. I could always buy more flowers if I wanted to.

These thoughts restored my balance and calm. When my partner got home, he immediately brought up the subject by apologizing for forgetting our share of the tulips at his mom's place. He'd taken all of them so she could help arrange them into two bouquets.

I was grateful for his explanation, but I'd reached a place where it didn't matter what had happened to them. The situation had provided me with an opportunity to practice a happiness skill and I was grateful for that.

In a Nutshell

Understanding that the conclusions your brain arrives at aren't always true is an important realization when it comes to happiness. Sometimes, when you think your life sucks, it really doesn't. Training yourself to question conclusions before embracing them can help your life be more peaceful and your relationships less tumultuous.

Small-step Strategy

The next time you notice yourself getting agitated about a situation, pause and follow the suggested steps.

- Slow down and breathe.

- Actively look for information that disproves your initial conclusion.

- Consider other possible explanations.

- Ask yourself whether your conclusion fits with what you know about the person or people involved in the situation.

- Remind yourself to keep things in perspective rather than overreacting.

THIRTY-FIVE

Make A Bad Day Better

As I was wandering through Costco recently, I was struck yet again by the increasing price of food. I was bothered by this thought more than usual. My feelings were further disturbed when, shortly after returning home, I received an email saying my Christmas flights to England had been canceled. I'd booked my tickets months ago and was looking forward to it more than I can explain. My already challenged feelings took another little nosedive.

Fortunately, I recognized that I was standing on a precipice. I could let these events take charge of my mood and sink into a "poor me" attitude, or I could choose to connect to happiness by viewing my circumstances with a more positive filter.

"The optimist sees the donut; the pessimist sees the hole."

Oscar Wilde

Here are a few ways you can make a bad day seem less horrible.

Limit your social media exposure.

Reading posts about the amazing things that are happening in other people's lives can cause your confidence to slump. Research suggests that the more time you spend on platforms like Facebook, the more likely it is that your self-esteem will drop.

Share your situation and ask for help.

You may feel vulnerable opening up to a friend or family member about the challenges in your life, but a trouble shared really is a trouble halved. Choose someone who'll listen with sympathy and compassion. They don't need to have a solution but listen to their wisdom with an open mind. If they offer to help, don't refuse because you don't want to inconvenience them. Acts of kindness are an amazing way to increase happiness. The giver gets as much positivity from helping as you will from receiving their assistance.

Be grateful.

Studies show that experiencing gratitude boosts feelings of wellbeing. Being thankful for the little things in life is just as important as appreciating the big stuff. It's easy to lose sight of this fact, especially when you feel like you're drowning in problems. Think about your cup of coffee, the roof over your head, or the people in your life. Spend a few minutes concentrating on the good things. They're there, even though they may not spring to mind immediately.

Tomorrow is a new day.

Things almost always look brighter after a good night's sleep. Hold on to that knowledge as you work your way through a bad day.

Do one thing you have control over.

This could be writing an email, making a call you've been avoiding, or crossing something else off your procrastination list. Even choosing to go for a walk or to eat more healthily will leave you with a greater sense of empowerment.

I can't control rising prices, or make WestJet reinstate my canceled booking. I can, however, choose what to spend my money on and contact the airline to see if they can put me on alternative flights.

As the world becomes less predictable, worry and disappointment can seem to be just a heartbeat away. Don't let the events that surround you sabotage your day. When life gives you lemons, appreciate the brightness of their color, breathe in the sweetness of their peel and then decide whether you want lemonade, lemon meringue pie or margaritas.

"Worry does not empty tomorrow of its sorrow; it empties today of its strength."

Corrie ten Boom

In a Nutshell

Remember that everything in life is a choice. You can wallow in self-pity and feel victimized by your day, or you can choose to embrace a positive perspective.

Small-step Strategy

When you feel like your day has developed a life of its own and you don't like where it's taking you, do something that you have control over. Get something off your to-do list, book tickets for a movie, or do some cooking. Anything that helps you feel empowered will enable you to view your bad day in a more positive light.

Thirty-six

Reduce Wrinkles with Kindness

I was reminded recently of just how many kind people there are in our community.

We were at Costco buying a storage shed. The box with the unassembled shed in it was incredibly big and heavy, so we had to get help loading it onto the flatbed. Once at the car, a new problem presented itself. The carton was too big to fit in the back of our vehicle. The only chance we had of getting it home was to put it on the roof rack. I'd been no help getting the box onto the trolley, so I was pretty sure there wasn't a chance in Hades that I'd be able to lift it above my head to place it onto the roof.

As we stood looking at our predicament, a man came by and offered to help. He took my place lifting the box onto the roof rack. The next step was to find a way to secure it. I went back into the store to find some cords. I returned with a package of rachet straps that were perfect for the task. The instructions on the back made the process look easy, but it wasn't. As we struggled to figure out how they worked, a fellow parked beside us and offered to help. His family stood patiently while he showed us how to work the rachets.

The kindness of these people came quickly and willingly, without us having to ask. I'm sure you'll agree this is a great story, but you might be wondering what any of this has to do with reducing wrinkles. Let's start down that path by talking about oxidation, free radicals, and antioxidants.

Your body is approximately sixty percent H20, or water. The H represents hydrogen and the O oxygen. Oxygen looks like two circles joined together by a bridge. If you want a visual, think of Harry Potter's glasses. Sometimes the bridge breaks and the oxygen atoms get separated. This turns them into free radicals.

Free radicals don't want to be single. They want to be part of a pair and will do pretty much anything to reestablish a relationship. If they can't find an appropriate atom, they'll link themselves to healthy cells in places like your skin, the lining of your arteries, your brain, or even your immune system, causing the healthy cells to break down. This is known as oxidation.

To get a better idea of what oxidation means, think about a slice of apple that's left out in the open. What happens to it? It turns brown. This is oxidation. When oxidation happens in your body, collagen breaks down and results in wrinkles, loose saggy skin, dark spots, and fine lines.

Oxidation is a natural process, but you may not want to encourage it to happen too early, or too quickly. To keep free radicals under control, the body uses something called antioxidants. As their name implies, they are against (anti) oxidization. Antioxidants are willing and able to partner with free radicals and can do this without damage to the body. If you have enough antioxidants to mop up the free radicals, you can slow the aging process.

You naturally have antioxidants in your body, but you can increase their population by eating certain foods. Kale, spinach, raspberries, blueberries, cinnamon, dark chocolate, green tea, and olive oil are all high in antioxidants.

Another way to limit oxidation is to increase the amount of oxytocin released by your brain. This is a feel-good hormone that you can't get from your diet. It has to be produced internally.

This is where kindness comes into the equation. Kind thoughts, actions, and feelings turn on an oxytocin tap in your brain, slowing down oxidative stress in your skin, muscles, arteries, and immune system.

You can also slow down oxidation by limiting the number of free radicals you have. Stress is a major contributor to breaking the bridge between oxygen atoms. Decreasing the amount of stress you experience is probably the best strategy, but if that's absolutely impossible, minimize its effect by breathing deeply, spending at least a few minutes surrounded by nature every day, exercising, hanging out with people you like, or being kind.

Being a kind person doesn't mean you won't age, but it will slow down the process. And remember, kindness shouldn't be reserved only for other people. It's also important to be kind to yourself and to animals.

In the words of novelist Henry James,

> *"Three things in human life are important. The first is to be kind. The second is to be kind. The third is to be kind."*

In a Nutshell

Acts of kindness are an easy way to connect more deeply with happiness and they don't have to be major. Small gestures are just as effective when it comes to reducing oxidation, and therefore wrinkles and aging.

Small-step Strategy

Draw your brain's attention to your desire to sprinkle kindness throughout your day. Consciously look for opportunities to do this. It can be as simple as opening a door for another person, reaching something down from a high shelf in the grocery store, or buying coffee for whoever's standing behind you at the coffee shop.

Thirty-seven

Talk About Your Favorite Subject

D o you talk to yourself? I do. When I was at university in Victoria, I found a mirror that said, "You can talk to me now. No one's looking." I bought it and proudly hung it in my room for all to see. It provided me with a huge sense of relief. Its existence suggested that I wasn't the only one to have conversations with myself.

Talking is the way I process my thoughts, so if there isn't anyone to talk with, I chat to myself. It isn't a behavior I developed consciously. It wasn't until my siblings teased me about it that I became aware I did it. They loved to remind me of the saying that talking to yourself is the first sign of madness. As a result, I tried to hide what I was doing. I wasn't very successful. When I was married, my husband said he always knew when I was upset or frustrated, because he could hear me muttering to myself.

I've become more comfortable over the years about owning who I am. I don't try to hide my personal conversations the way I once did. It helps that anyone who passes me in the car probably assumes I'm talking on the phone, not to myself. Despite this increase in self-acceptance, I felt comforted when I stumbled upon an article called *The Neuroscience of Everybody's Favourite Topic*. Yes, we all have the same thing we love to talk about. Ourselves!

According to the research outlined in this article, when you're having a conversation, about 60 percent of what you say will be about you. That impressive statistic rises to 80 percent if you are communicating on social media. The researchers from the Harvard University Social Cognitive and Affective Neuroscience Lab wanted to see what parts of the brain became active when subjects talked about themselves rather than about other people. They discovered that talking about yourself activates the same areas of the brain as sex, cocaine, and good food. You talk about yourself because it feels good.

So, what does this have to do with talking to yourself? The scientists took their study one step further. They wanted to know if someone needed to listen when you talk about yourself for it to be a pleasurable experience.

As someone who talks to herself, this caught my attention. I'm pretty sure my conversations usually center around me. Do I get subconscious pleasure from this habit?

This time, each participant brought a friend or relative with them who was asked to go into an adjoining room. Before subjects were asked questions about themselves or others, they were told whether their response would be live broadcast to the person they brought with them, or kept private, even from the research team. In other words, sometimes what they were saying was shared and sometimes they were talking only to themselves. The study discovered that talking to yourself about you creates a strong hit of pleasure, although not as intense as when you're talking to someone else about you.

I no longer have my mirror from university, but I have a plaque that's almost as good. It says, "Of course, I talk to myself. Sometimes I need expert advice."

In a Nutshell

Talking about yourself makes you feel good, regardless of who you're communicating with. Don't worry if you don't have anyone to talk to. Consider going to your mirror and having a conversation with someone who loves to hear about you, just as much as you do.

Small-step Strategy

The next time you need a mood boost:

- Get out a photo album and write, think, or talk about your memories.

- Journal about what's going on in your life.

- Have a conversation with your reflection in the mirror.

THIRTY-EIGHT

Learn From Your Mistakes

When I taught Microsoft Office classes, I'd tell my students that I loved it when they made mistakes. I'd move joyfully over to the person that was having trouble and thank them for admitting something had gone wrong. Their problem helped the entire class learn. We'd work together as a team to figure out what the problem was and how to fix it. If at a future time someone else had the same issue, they'd already have an idea how to remedy it.

You may well be thanking your lucky stars that you never had me as an instructor, because you hate having attention drawn to your mistakes and challenges. If this is the case, you may well have been programed to believe that getting it right the first time is the definition of success. If this is the case, you aren't alone.

School-age children are often praised more frequently for their lack of mistakes. Although this may seem like a good thing, needing to get it right on your first attempt can encourage people to avoid challenges in case they aren't successful. Of course, there's nothing wrong with getting the right answer on your first attempt. Just be aware that you learn more when you get things wrong than when the right solution comes easily the first time.

In the case of a program like Excel or Word, things are bound to go wrong at least occasionally, especially when you're first getting started. If you make a mistake and then figure out how to fix it, your level of understanding will expand. When it comes to errors, the key is to avoid repeating the same mistakes, not escape making new ones. When mistake avoidance is your motivation, you aren't open to the valuable information that comes with those blunders.

Research shows you need to be open to making errors in order to appreciate the underlying concepts necessary to deepen your understanding. Evidence based research suggests that people learn better if they make mistakes on their way to getting the correct answers. Rather than seeing feedback as negative criticism, view it as an opportunity to improve and learn.

Success doesn't come from being right the first time, it's about discovering new skills and information. Mistakes aren't failures. They're a guide to what still needs to be learned. As Thomas Edison said, "I have not failed. I've just found 10,000 ways that won't work."

In a Nutshell

Accepting mistakes doesn't mean you have to love them, but you need to know in your soul that it's okay to make them. You're going to stumble and screw up from time to time. That's just part of being human. Life shouldn't be about avoiding mistakes or feeling ashamed of the ones you make, but about learning from them so you don't make the same ones again.

Small-step Strategy

Take responsibility for your mistakes.

Learn from them, and if necessary, forgive yourself and anyone else who was involved, then move on with the knowledge that you're a little bit wiser as a result.

I find that sharing my mistakes with a loving friend or family member helps me with this skill.

Download your free copy of the Affirmations and Reflection Prompts for each chapter.

ReenRose.com/FreeResource

THIRTY-NINE

Create and Maintain Boundaries

When I first moved into my former house, I had the back yard landscaped. I had what's known as a bare land strata. I owned my house and the surrounding property, but it was maintained and overseen by a strata council. I wasn't quite sure where the boundary between my place and the house next to me was, so I only landscaped the section that was obviously mine. That left a segment in the middle like no man's land.

I'm sure part of it was mine, but I don't know exactly how much. I spoke with my neighbor about it, but we had different ideas of where the boundary was. That wouldn't have happened if there was a fence or visible boundary between our houses. Like Robert Frost once said, "Good fences make good neighbors."

When you know exactly where your property ends and the next one starts, it's easier to avoid confusion and disagreements. This principle also applies to your life.

Take, for example, the idea of personal space. How do you feel when a stranger or someone you don't really like stands very close to you? It can be extremely uncomfortable. They're invading your personal space.

Just how close someone has to be before you feel uneasy varies from person to person. There's no rule about what area around you is yours. Whatever the size, a healthy boundary is one that states no one should enter your space without an invitation. If they do, you can choose to let them remain there, step back to re-establish your space, or tell them they're too close.

I find negativity draining, and I have a boundary around it. My family and good friends all know this about me. I can only be in negative energy for so long. Then I'll tune out or walk away.

UK-based psychologist Dr. Tara Quinn-Cirillo defines having personal boundaries as knowing how to separate your feelings, or "stuff," from someone else's.

"As human beings, we have our own thoughts, memories and lived experiences, and sometimes that can become very blurred with someone else's," she says. "Boundaries are healthy for helping you identify and keep that space."

Healthy personal boundaries also help promote a sense of autonomy. That means you feel a level of control over your life. Rather than being a victim to the actions and desires of others, you get to establish what is and isn't acceptable for you. Doing this is empowering and can help keep confusion to a minimum.

Setting boundaries is about communicating what's right for you when it comes to how you want to be treated, and what things you're willing to do. It can take courage to create boundaries, especially if you're not used to establishing them. Start small. Notice when your energy is being drained by a person or situation. This is where a boundary needs to be established. What change can you make to limit or eliminate that sense of depletion?

It's important to recognize that these invisible lines have multiple benefits. As well as communicating the behaviors you're willing to accept from others, they help the people you interact with to understand what behaviors they can expect from you. If you don't want people hugging you, you're unlikely to hug them, either. A clear boundary will help others to understand this about you.

These also make it easier to identify when someone has stepped over the line. You don't wonder if you're imagining your feelings of discomfort or frustration when you know where your line is.

In a Nutshell

Creating and maintaining clear boundaries will help you nurture physical, mental, and emotional health. Without them, you can get sucked into the exhaustive behaviors of others. This can lead to fatigue and a slump in wellbeing.

Small-step Strategy

How good are you at creating and maintaining healthy boundaries? This is an important question to ask yourself. Be honest. If you struggle, you can learn to be better. Start small. Choose one boundary you could establish that would make you happier, and therefore healthier?

FORTY

Balance Certainty with Surprise

Balance: a condition in which different elements are equal or in the correct proportions.

Oxford Dictionary

Over the years, there's been a lot of discussion and research about the importance of achieving work/life balance, but that isn't the only area of your world that requires equilibrium if you want to be happy.

Humans have a need for both certainty and uncertainty. Too much or too little of either can cause problems and leave you feeling frustrated.

Certainty helps you feel safe. You know what to expect and can prepare yourself for what lies ahead. Studies show that people would rather know they're going to lose their job than think it's a possibility. Certain doom is preferable to possible disaster. I guess that explains why it's so hard to wait to find out whether an application for a job, university position, or contest is successful. Wondering what might or might not happen throws you out of the safety that comes with certainty.

However, uncertainty has its own charm. It offers the mystery and magic of possibility. Wondering what unexpected things might unfold is part of the excitement of life.

Humans are awash with contradiction. You want to feel safe, but not too safe. Too much certainty leads to boredom, just like too much uncertainty causes anxiety and fear. Getting the balance right between these two states can be tricky.

Keep healthy habits like writing in a journal and exercising as part of a regular routine, but add some variety by choosing to write in different environments and vary your fitness activities. Try a new hobby, call someone you haven't talked to in a while, or change the order you do your daily chores. One of my favorite strategies when life becomes too predictable is to write the tasks for the day on pieces of paper and put them into a container. Instead of doing everything in the same predictable sequence, I draw the slips out to create a random order.

If you work from home or are self-employed, it's important to establish boundaries around your weekends. Choose a few things that you will only do on Saturdays and Sundays. This will help to differentiate those days from the rest of the week.

Increase your enjoyment of life, by ensuring you experience both certainty and surprise on a daily basis.

In a Nutshell

You have the ability connect with more happiness by finding a better balance between certainty and novelty. Anything that adds a flair of mystery and encourages a level of uncertainty will help combat boredom, just like grounding yourself in the things you know for sure will make you feel safe and secure.

Small-step Strategy

If you find yourself worrying about the future, remind yourself of all the things you're certain of. Think about your friends and family, your skills and abilities, and times in the past when you survived challenges. State all the things you know for sure.

Humans love routine, but only to a point. If you're feeling bored with the familiar pattern of your day-to-day existence, you may know too many things for certain. This is the case if you wake up and you're pretty sure you know exactly how your day will unfold.

If you have too much certainty, try adding a little more spontaneity and mystery. This will help break up any monotony that may have developed.

FORTY-ONE

Believe You Can

I recently came across a reference to the story *The Little Engine That Could* by Arnold Munk. My mind immediately flashed back to my childhood. I could see myself sitting in our living room in Saskatchewan as my mom read this story to me. I can still hear her voice in my head as she repeated, "I think I can. I think I can. I think I can." This is a vivid memory considering I was only six when we left the prairies.

If you aren't familiar with the story, it's about a train that's having a very bad day. It's trying to get to the town on the other side of the mountain, but it breaks down before it gets there. A steep incline is between it and its destination. Large engines are asked to pull the train to the town, but for one reason or another, they all refuse. The last hope of getting the cars to the other side rests with a small engine used to moving cars around the train station tracks. When asked, instead of saying no like all the others, it agrees to attempt the task.

All the way up the mountain it repeats to itself, "I think I can. I think I can. I think I can." When it reaches the top and starts its descent, the mantra changes to, "I thought I could. I thought I could." This little engine did what none of the bigger and more powerful ones would even attempt.

This may be a children's book, but the message applies equally to people of all ages. Imagine living a life where you aren't afraid to challenge yourself, and you believe in your ability to do anything you choose? I can think of many times in my life when I was afraid that I wouldn't measure up, so I didn't even try.

My two siblings were thought to be the smart ones in the family. I was the social one. The last thing I wanted to do was prove everyone right by trying my hardest in school and not doing as well as my brother and sister. I worked hard enough to get respectable grades, but I certainly didn't do more than that. I chose the mantra, "I'm afraid I can't, so I won't bother trying." I was just like the big engines in the story.

I passionately believe that many of the limitations that stop you are of your own making. It's easy to let a bad experience take over and spoil what could have been something amazing.

I was speaking with a friend who recounted how she tried out for the cheerleading squad when she was a teenager. She made it through the first round of selection, but decided to drop out because she didn't think she'd be able to afford everything that went along with being a cheerleader. Rather than believing in herself and her ability to find a way to make it work, she gave up.

I could relate to her story. I've done the same thing myself. I've created the limitations and then stopped trying. Those days are gone. I now know that I can do anything I choose to do. I've learned not to pay too much attention to what others think of my endeavors. I've found people who believe in me when I'm struggling to believe in myself. I remind myself of Kanter's Law: things always look like a failure in the middle.

It is never too late to create a life of possibilities rather than limitations. You're a survivor. If you set your mind on something, you can make it happen. The only one that can stop you is you. If you aren't used to living a life of possibilities, that might seem preposterous. But stop for a minute and think about it. You are human. All humans are survivors. If you need to make something work, you'll figure it out.

That doesn't mean it'll be easy, or without challenges, but you can make it happen if you want it badly enough. Instead of limiting yourself, adopt the attitude of the little engine in the story. Keep telling yourself, "I think I can." If you want to be bold, change it to, "I know I can." You might even want to throw in a few train noises to give yourself encouragement.

I wonder what life would be like if you believed you could do anything you put your mind to, or at the very least weren't afraid to try. A life where you're willing to reach for the stars even if you don't succeed is bound to be richer than limiting yourself through fear of failure.

In a Nutshell

You'll never know how you feel about something or whether you can do it until you try. Don't limit yourself by refusing to even attempt it.

Small-step Strategy

The next time you notice yourself declining a challenge or being afraid to try something new, ask yourself why. Is it a limiting idea that's holding you back? What will happen if you try and don't succeed? Will it be the end of the world as you know it? Rather than giving up, become tenacious. Make *"I think I can"* your new mantra.

FORTY-TWO

Accept Change

I do some of my best writing in coffee shops. I'm not sure what makes them such fertile environments for my thoughts, but they are. Perhaps it is because I'm separated from work and domestic distractions, or maybe it's because they're a buzz of energy.

Regardless of the reason, when I want to create some great content, I grab my laptop and walk to my neighborhood java joint. The walk is a great opportunity to organize my thoughts, so I don't spend too much of my writing time thinking.

I have a habit of heading to my favorite coffee shop on the same day each week, but for scheduling reasons, I had to write on a different day than usual one time. I purchased my coffee and then went into the back to get settled. As I made my way to my favorite corner and its comfy chair, a problem presented itself. Someone was sitting in my usual place. I felt off balance and momentarily wondered if I should just turn around and go home. But after a brief look of disbelief, I heaved a sigh and chose a different spot.

Has this ever happened to you? Have you imagined a situation that didn't pan out the way you expected?

Some people are born with a natural affinity for change. They look forward to it with anticipation. They're masters of going with the flow. Others are lovers of routine and familiarity. When change comes their way, they try to avoid making eye contact with it, in the futile hope that it'll pass them by.

You might be like me and enjoy new experiences, but only when you choose them. This leads you to believe you're somehow in control of what's happening. It took me a long time to realize that was just an illusion.

Regardless of how you respond to change, you can't escape it. It's one of the few things you can count on. Nothing stays the same forever no matter how much you may want it to. You can resist all you want, but you can rarely stop it from happening. Happy people may not love change, but they're accepting of it. At the very least, this is what you should aim for. Allow things to shift without trying to hold them in place.

I recommend you spend a few minutes examining your relationship with new situations and experiences. If you only shift your behaviors, perspectives, and routines when you you're forced into it, it may be time to choose to step out of your comfort zone. The more you do so, the easier it'll become.

I used to imagine comfort zones as islands that you might take a holiday from, but could always return to when you got tired of being uncomfortable. With age and wisdom, this picture has changed. Now I imagine life as a continuous journey, or a route with ever-changing terrain. Sometimes it's sandy, then it goes steeply up hill, only to become muddy as you reach the top. Eventually it becomes sandy again. Although the sensation feels weird after the rocky path you've been traveling, you adjust more quickly because it's something you've experienced before.

The only way you can keep the surface under your feet the same is to stand still, or march on the spot. You may not feel the discomfort of new sensation by doing this, but a different problem may arise. Staying in the same place is likely to become boring and monotonous. It's why walking outside is usually more interesting than being on a treadmill.

As you learn to accept change, it becomes easier to navigate. It becomes a natural part of life. You may even feel more at peace, as you're not wasting energy on resistance.

If learning to accept change is something you want to practice, here are a few things to consider.

- Think of times in your life when you've found yourself out of your comfort zone and survived. If you did it once, you can do it again. The first time is often the most challenging. It gets easier with subsequent experiences. Some of the best things in life come as the result of being forced out of your comfort zone. Humans may enjoy routine, but they equally love unexpected surprises. Not knowing what's around the next corner is one of life's greatest gifts.

- Don't leave too much time between your ventures into the unknown. If you wait too long between unfamiliar experiences, it will feel like the first time over and over again.

- Begin by inviting change into your life on your own terms. You can do this by changing your schedule or choosing a different route to work, the store, or for a walk. Instead of doing your laundry on Tuesday, try completing it on Friday. Challenge yourself to sit at a different table in the coffee shop, until you've sat at them all.

- When unexpected change presents itself, rather than greeting it with a doom-and-gloom attitude, look for something positive in it. Optimism might not be your first response, but that's okay as long as you get there in the end. As I sat in the coffee shop looking over at my usual chair, I noticed two men sitting at a table beside it. They were having an unusually loud conversation. I realized that if I'd been sitting beside them, it would have been much harder to concentrate. Having to sit in a different place turned out to be a blessing in disguise.

Take time to get comfortable with being uncomfortable. This mindset is a major contributor to inner peace.

In a Nutshell

Every time an opportunity for change presents itself, remember that it's gifting you with the chance to practice being more adaptable and flexible. These are important skills to develop if you want your life to be a happy one, regardless of what's happening around you.

Small-step Strategy

What's one thing you can do differently today? Bonus points if it's something you aren't excited about, but you know will be beneficial.

FORTY-THREE

Suffering Is Optional

"Only we humans worry about the future, regret the past,
and blame ourselves for the present. We get frustrated when
we can't have what we want, and disappointed when what
we like ends. We suffer that we suffer. We get upset about
being in pain, angry about dying, sad about waking up sad
yet another day. This kind of suffering – which
encompasses most of our unhappiness and dissatisfaction –
is constructed by the brain. It is made up."

Rick Hanson, Ph.D.

This is an excerpt from the book *Buddha's Brain*. It is one of those passages that comes along every once in a while, and refuses to be forgotten.

You suffer because your mind chooses to suffer.
Think about it for a minute. Re-read the excerpt again. Think some more.

My first reaction was disbelief. Why would the brain of a happiness maven choose to suffer? But when I considered that most suffering comes from worrying about the future and replaying negative events from the past, the truth became clear. I don't have to spend my time thinking about disastrous events that may never happen, or dwell on past experiences I can do nothing about. This suffering is an activity of choice, albeit not necessarily conscious choice.

I can't count the number of times I've counselled my children to stop worrying about something that may never happen. It's good advice, but easier said than done, especially if you don't notice you're doing it, or if you have an anxiety disorder. In the latter case, I recommend speaking with a professional if you're struggling.

I'm not suggesting you can avoid worry completely, but there's a difference between worrying about something that's currently happening, versus something that might never happen. One is the reality of the present, while the other is the unknown future. It's the latter that I suggest you work to avoid.

When the recession of the 1980s hit, layoffs were common. I had just started my teaching career and knew I was at risk. Worrying that I might get laid off is suffering that was avoidable, although I didn't realize that at the time. Worrying about how I would pay my bills after the layoff notice arrived was something my brain needed to work through. Dealing with the present is necessary; worrying about the future is optional.

Why does your brain choose to make you suffer by running through possible negative scenarios that might never happen? This is an evolutionary survival strategy. As your number one drive is survival, the brain discovered it could gain an advantage by thinking about possible danger scenarios that might arise and then creating ways to deal with them. You would not only have thought of possible solutions if the situation ever arose, but you'd also have mentally practiced them.

Similarly, the human brain discovered it could reinforce already proven survival strategies by replaying them over and over. This is the basis of why you dwell on negative events from the past. You probably don't enjoy revisiting these experiences, but because they're examples of survival techniques that worked, replaying them is your mind's way of reinforcing the learning so you can use that strategy again. There may be no use crying over spilled milk, but your brain encourages you to do it anyway.

These evolutionary survival strategies often run in the background of your life, a little like the anti-virus software on your computer. Unless your attention is drawn to it, you've probably forgotten it's there.

Now that you know what your mind is up to, you can take steps to lessen your suffering by spending as much time as possible living in the present.

In a Nutshell

"If you are depressed, you are living in the past.

If you are anxious, you are living in the future.

If you are at peace, you are living in the present."

Lao Tzu

Small-step Strategy

The next time you find yourself worrying about the future or reliving painful experiences of the past, be aware of what's happening. Rather than telling yourself to stop being so silly or to get over it, show yourself compassion.

Compassion is defined by the Mirriam-Webster online dictionary as "sympathetic consciousness of others' distress together with a desire to alleviate it." Instead of scolding yourself, imagine you're helping a child and say something soothing. Physical actions strengthen feelings, so put your hand on your heart or your cheek while you speak to yourself. You don't have to say the words aloud, saying them in your mind is just as effective.

FORTY-FOUR

Join the Dots Differently

Have you ever been in a situation where someone made a wrong assumption about you? While on a vacation with my friend, this happened to me twice in a twelve-hour period.

Assumption: something you accept as true without question or proof.

Cambridge Dictionary

As I signed us both into the pool at the hotel we were staying at, the man taking the information assumed I was my friend's mother. Yes, I'm old enough to have given birth to her, but I didn't. The next morning, I happened to step into the elevator at the same time as a man I didn't know. We were soon joined by a third person who struck up a conversation that made it clear he thought we were a couple.

The human brain likes to make sense of the world. Give it a few dots and it will join them together. It isn't really concerned whether the conclusion it draws is true or not. You may think you understand why a person made a specific decision, took a particular course of action, or uttered certain words, but do you really?

Everybody makes assumptions, but they're sneaky. You probably don't even notice you're doing it. If a car speeds past you, you may assume the driver's an idiot. But maybe they're rushing someone to the hospital.

Assumptions are typically based on past experiences and desires, rather than facts and evidence. The biggest problem with assumptions is that you use them to make judgements and decisions.

Believing you won't be considered for a job you want might stop you from applying for it. Thinking a co-worker doesn't like you can affect how you feel about going to work. Assuming your romantic partner isn't in love with you anymore has the potential to make you pull away.

I know that I make assumptions, but I don't always recognize I'm doing it. On the same holiday I talked about earlier, my attention was drawn to this topic when my friend and I were floating in the ocean. We saw something bobbing in the water in front of us and assumed it was a log. It wasn't until someone asked us if we'd seen the turtles that we realized it wasn't driftwood that was floating in front of us, but a beautiful sea turtle. Our initial assumption stopped us from looking closer at the object in the water. The experience reminded us to be more observant and not jump to conclusions so quickly.

In personal development, awareness is the first step to transformation.

In a Nutshell

Because your brain always wants the world to make sense, it takes information and develops stories around it. But the conclusions it draws aren't always correct. By being aware of this tendency, you can avoid jumping to conclusions too quickly.

Small-step Strategy

The next time you notice you've arrived at a conclusion about someone or something, stop and ask yourself, "How do I know that? Do I have evidence, or is my brain joining dots haphazardly to make a story?"

List the facts you know for sure and then take a minute to see if they support the conclusion you arrived at initially. Consider whether there's an alternative explanation.

FORTY-FIVE

Look Temptation in the Face

I'm not sure how I attract, and am attracted to, men who have great metabolisms and can eat pretty much anything they want without gaining weight. I'm not so lucky. When I lived on my own it was easier to deal with temptation. I could avoid unwanted calories by not having tantalizing food and drink in the house. I didn't have to see delectable treats when I opened a cupboard or endure the aroma of bacon.

Tempt: to entice to do wrong by promise of pleasure or gain.

Merriam-Webster Dictionary

It's interesting that temptation has traditionally been linked to the idea of sin or doing something wrong. Is it really fair to consider having a second piece of pie a transgression? I think it makes more sense to view temptation as an incompatibility between something you want and goals you've set for yourself.

A bag of Cheezies may taste good, but it won't help you achieve your desire to be slimmer or healthier. If you're trying to save enough money for a downpayment, spending cash on something that isn't absolutely necessary feels off because you know it isn't moving you towards your chosen goal.

Avoidance is a strategy, but not one that encourages you to enjoy life to its fullest. Missing out on valuable experiences because you say no to offers of dinners out or catching up over a beverage isn't the answer.

Some people are more prone to cravings than others, but everybody has specific areas of weakness. Temptation is often associated with food, but it can just as easily be time on your phone or skipping exercise in favor of inactivity.

Humans have a limited amount of self-control, although some people have more than others. You probably know where you sit in that scale. Regardless of how much impulse control you have naturally, one of the best things you can do to battle temptation is to be aware of its existence.

Temptation is intricately intertwined with the brain's reward system. A rodent study discovered that rats that were more prone to temptation experienced a dopamine spike when presented with the cue for food. In other words, they received feel-good hormones from the brain when they thought food was on its way. These studies also revealed that rodents that experienced more stress when they were young were more likely to have difficulty with temptation when they were fully grown.

So, if temptation is part of life, what's the best way to combat it?

- Practice self-awareness and mindfulness. Meditation is one way to do this, as it's been shown to increase mindfulness and help regulate emotions.

- Establish healthy habits. These are instrumental in resisting temptation. Eat regular meals, have an exercise regime, and plan when you'll spend time on devices.

- Replace "no" with "not now." Choosing not to indulge at this moment doesn't mean you'll never have another opportunity. If you're desperate for chocolate, have it earlier in the day rather than in the evening.

- Find an accountability partner. Having a buddy to share your struggles, victories, and exercise classes with increases your chances of success.

Few people have life paths that look like a Roman road. There will be twists and turns and that's okay.

In a Nutshell

Giving in to temptation isn't wrong or sinful. It's a choice. But you'll feel more connected to happiness if the majority of your decisions are in alignment with your goals and values.

Small-step Strategy

Managing temptation doesn't mean relying completely on abstinence or avoidance. Look for moderation rather than an all or nothing approach. What's one small thing you could do to help you change your behavior?

FORTY-SIX

Avoid Energy Vampires

When I say that coffee shops are one of my favourite places to write, I know I'm in good company. J.K. Rowling created her Harry Potter masterpiece in coffee shops in Scotland. I think it's the atmosphere they contain that makes them such a good environment for writers. Regardless of whether it's the morning rush or an afternoon lull, their energy is stimulating.

Personal and collective energy of this type comes from a variety of sources, including physical, mental, and emotional well-being. The healthier your lifestyle, the more likely you are to have good energy. Having good social connections and personal relationships will also contribute to the quality of your energy. These things are all within your control. If you're suffering from lack of energy, go outside for a walk, improve your diet, exercise more, or nurture your relationships.

Fortunately, or unfortunately, you're not an island. When you interact with others, you're susceptible to their energy. Energy transfers between people who are in close proximity. Have you ever walked into a room and immediately felt uneasy? This is energy at work. You absorb the collective feelings of the people you spend time with. Surrounding yourself with dissatisfied co-workers will lead to a greater level of discontent. Spending the evening with complaining friends will encourage you to feel less satisfied with your life. Talking to your depressed cousin will leave you feeling drained.

Limiting the amount of time you spend with these sorts of people is one way of dealing with energy vampires, but it isn't always a practical one. I come from a family that's riddled with mood disorders, so unless I want to cut ties with people who are important to me, that isn't the answer.

Instead, arm yourself with some strategies to help you protect your positive energy.

Boost your energy

Before you spend time with people who carry negative energy, make sure you are in prime energetic condition. Go for a walk, meditate, or watch a feel-good movie.

Overwhelm their energy with yours

By ensuring you're feeling positive, you can spread your vibe to them instead of simply absorbing theirs. If you're aware of what's happening, you can consciously work toward making this happen.

Limit the amount of time you spend around negative energy

Look for signs that you're beginning to feel less energized and take that as an indication that it's time to leave. If it's a family member who's affecting you, little and often may be better than lots occasionally.

Take reinforcements with you

If you're meeting someone who tends to be negative, including a colleague or friend who radiates positive energy can combine with yours to make the experience less draining. This is a variation on the "overwhelming their energy with yours" theme.

Know when to cut ties

If you have family members who bear a strong energetic similarity to Eeyore, you may not want to cut them out of your life, but friends who you dread seeing, or work colleagues that leave you frustrated and low, may not be the best choice of people to spend time with. Not all friends will be in your life forever, and though it's a tough thing to do, making the decision to spend less or no time with people who are constantly complaining or criticizing may be the kindest thing you can do for yourself.

Cleanse your energy

When you finish your time around low-energy people, consciously take time to cleanse the negative by doing something you know helps you regain your positivity.

Become more mindful of your energy

Check in with it regularly throughout the day. If it is lagging, do something to lift it. Don't wait until you hit rock bottom. This is what tends to happen when you're unconscious of your energy and how it's affected by others.

In a Nutshell

We all know someone who attracts people the minute they walk into a room. They may be a stranger, but you feel pulled to be in their physical space. This is usually because the energy they carry is extremely positive. Humans don't want to feel low, or depressed. If you can raise your vibration by being in the company of someone who carries a vibrant aura, you're likely to find an opportunity to approach them, or at least be in their proximity. This is another reason to foster your own strongly positive energy.

It will mean you can brighten someone else's life just by spending time with them.

Small-step Strategy

The type of energy you exude is largely within your control. You can choose whether to glow with positivity or be like Charlie Brown's friend, Pig Pen, and carry around a cloud of negativity.

You may not give your personal energy a lot of thought, but it's important to be aware of it if you want to create a life and relationships that you love. Consciously check in with how you feel, several times a day. Is your current energy positive or negative? If you need help remembering, set a timer or reminder on your phone, or check in every time you visit the bathroom.

FORTY-SEVEN

Step Away from Gossip

I'm sure I'm not alone when I admit to talking to friends and family about other people. Sometimes it's to share information, and other times it's to express opinions about them and their choices. I don't deliberately set out to dissect these people or their lives, but conversations have a funny habit of taking on a life and direction of their own.

You may start by sharing a problem you're having, or a recent situation you've experienced. After all, doesn't a trouble shared become a trouble halved? The difficulty comes when you discuss issues and problems about someone the other person may or may not know, and who isn't actually participating in the conversation. When this happens, you may find yourself taking a step into the Gossip Zone.

The Cambridge dictionary defines gossip as: "Conversation or reports about other people's private lives that might be unkind, disapproving, or not true." Research both supports and condemns gossip. Some studies claim that gossip strengthens ties in social and business networks, while other research suggests it harms relationships.

I believe that, although you can wile away many hours gossiping, it isn't a happiness boosting activity. Participating in it might make you feel part of the group, or your ego may delight in believing that others are worse off, or lesser, than you. However, these reasons don't fit with the principles for creating a robust, happy life.

There's a fine line between sharing information about another person, and gossip. I believe the difference lies in the intention behind the conversation in question. If you're sharing information for a loving reason, like passing along an unbiased version of a situation, then I personally wouldn't consider the conversation gossip.

Sharing the fact that a friend has miscarried might help others keep from constantly talking about babies, or how difficult their births were. Knowing that someone has just been left by their partner may help you understand why they're behaving "out of character."

If you and a colleague talk about a boss who's micromanaging you, and making your lives at work extremely difficult, that might not be gossip depending on your intention. If you're trying to understand this person better, find ways to deal with your difficult working conditions, or simply sharing your frustration, you're probably not in the Gossip Zone.

However, if your intention is to share everything you know about your boss, regardless of who you heard it from, just so you can take delight in talking about all the ways they're a jerk, that's probably gossip.

When you gossip, your stories are often colored by your opinions. You put your own spin or interpretation on the events rather than stating facts. I wish I could say that I've never gossiped about other people, but sadly, that's not the case. I know how addictive this pastime can be, and how it can make you feel like you belong to the group you're gossiping with.

As a self-proclaimed happiness maven, I've come to realize that gossip doesn't foster true happiness, especially when you consider the principles happy people try to live their lives with. These include:

- Not judging other people, unless their actions directly affect you, or someone's in danger of getting hurt.

- Focusing on positives rather than negatives.

- Giving other people the benefit of the doubt, rather than believing that they're deliberately selfish, unthinking, or nasty.

- Not comparing yourself to other people, especially when the intention is to feel better about yourself.

- Accepting that everyone is on their own journey and has their own lessons to learn.

So, what do you do when you have a friend or family member who likes to gossip? You can't control the actions of others, so to believe it's your responsibility to change their gossiping ways is unrealistic, and not your place. You can only make the choice for yourself.

If you find yourself entering the Gossip Zone, here are a few strategies you can try:

- Change the current subject of conversation to something more positive/less gossipy.

- Explain that you prefer not to talk about people you don't know, or people who are not present to give their point of view.

- Suggest alternative, kinder reasons why the person being discussed acted the way they did.

- Remind your companions that information often changes drastically as it's passed from one person to another. Try playing a game of Gossip/Whispers, to illustrate this fact.

- Walk away; a quick trip to the bathroom can be a lifesaver at times like this.

In a Nutshell

Gossip may feel good in the moment, but it doesn't foster happiness. What's happening in other people's lives, for the most part, is none of your business. By understanding the intention behind your conversation, you can begin to determine whether you're sharing information or gossiping.

> ### Small-step Strategy
>
> When you find yourself talking about other people, stop and ask yourself what your intention is. If you notice that you're entering the Gossip Zone, step out of it, and surround yourself with vibrations that are more positive.

FORTY-EIGHT

Consider Ancient Wisdom

When I was in university, several of my friends were philosophy majors. Their reason for choosing a degree in philosophy was a complete mystery to me. Why would you study the words of ancient wisdom when you could be taking a degree that would lead to a profession in education, law, or engineering?

It's only with age that I've come to appreciate the positive influences that can be found in the words and practices of these ancient philosophers, or how timeless their thoughts were.

Philosophy itself literally means "love of wisdom."

When a new calendar year starts or a major life event happens, you may find yourself taking time to reflect on your life and the world. It's a way to find wisdom that can help you move forward.

With that thought in mind, I want to share some ancient wisdom that feels as relevant today as it did hundreds of years ago.

"We suffer more often in imagination than in reality."

Seneca (4 BC – AD 65)
Advisor to Roman Emperor Nero.

My mom used to tell me to *"Cross that bridge when you come to it."* It was her way of advising me not to worry about stuff that might never happen. Bad days appear easily enough without us dwelling on the *possibility* of a difficult day.

When challenges happen, you deal with them. For the most part, you have no other choice. If your dishwasher breaks, you get it fixed or start doing your dishes by hand. Worrying that it's old and might break serves no useful purpose. It could keep running for years.

"Men are disturbed not by things, but by the view which they take of them."

Epictetus (AD 50 – 135)
Born a slave.
Lived in Rome until he was banished.

Your brain receives information from your senses. Because it likes the world around you to make sense, it assigns meaning to the things you've seen, heard, smelled, touched, or felt. Smelling smoke doesn't necessarily mean danger, although that may be the first thought that comes into your mind.

If you see a friend scowling at you, your brain may jump to the conclusion that they're mad at you. But just because that's the first story your brain creates, it doesn't mean it's accurate. You get to choose a different perspective if you want.

Maybe they just had a disagreement with their partner, or received annoying news from their boss. There's every chance that the look on their face has absolutely nothing to do with you.

Just because your brain quickly assigns meaning to the information it receives doesn't mean you have to believe its interpretation without question. If the initial story disturbs you, choose a different one.

"I have often wondered how it is that every man loves himself more than all the rest of men, but yet sets less value on his own opinions of himself than on the opinions of others."

Marcus Aurelius (AD 161-180)
Roman emperor.

The truth of these words strikes me every time I read them. Why is it that we give so much power to the words of others? You may leave your home feeling like a million dollars, but it only takes one negative comment from another person to send you into a whirlwind of doubt.

There's an evolutionary reason for this. In primitive times, it was vital that humans worked together if they wanted to survive. One way of ensuring that this happened was for individuals to buy into the opinions and behaviors of the group as a whole.

If you rebelled, you were banished. That action was akin to death because it was virtually impossible to survive by yourself.

Caring more about the opinions of the group served humans when they roamed the savannah, but we've moved on since then. This is just one example of an outdated program that modern humans carry. If you want to break free from this obsolete behavior, the first step is to become aware that it exists.

It's unlikely that being aware of your tendency to take the opinions of others to heart will stop that behavior in its tracks, but it can help you make better decisions. Rather than assuming they must be right, you can pause and think about it with a clearer mind.

Perhaps there was a reason for their comment, or maybe you were reading more into it than they intended. In the end, it's your opinion that really matters.

Go back to the words of Seneca and choose a perspective that brings you peace. Amazingly, his wisdom and that of many of the other ancient philosophers is as applicable to life today as it was when their words were first recorded.

In a Nutshell

Reflection is the way adults learn. It's something that'll make your life richer and keep your brain in good condition.

Small-step Strategy

Choose the words of one of the ancient philosophers and think about what they were trying to say. How does this statement relate to your life or our modern world? Would you change it in some way to make it more applicable to you? Can you think of a time when you wish you'd used their wisdom?

If you like to journal or want to start journaling practice, these quotes can make great prompts.

FORTY-NINE

Connect With Yourself

Have you ever been in a situation that left you wanting the
ground to open and swallow you up? Of course, you have.
You're human.

Some people are more easily embarrassed than others. For
many years, I was one of those people. I think it's because I was
raised to care too much about what other people thought of me. I
was trying to be the person I believed I should be, rather than who
I really am. That person needed to be kept from view.

I learned to deal with embarrassment when I was in my
twenties. I started to use these experiences as dinner party
entertainment. No situation was too mortifying to share with my
friends, who laughed uproariously. Everybody loves to hear about
another person's cringe-worthy experiences. We can all relate and
imagine ourselves in a similar situation.

Sometimes I wonder if I'd be so quick to share things that I'm
truly ashamed of.

This thought emerged when I discovered that embarrassment
is a mild version of shame. According to the Merriam-Webster
dictionary, shame as "a painful emotion caused by consciousness
of guilt, shortcoming, or impropriety." In other words, shame

surfaces when you say or do something that re-enforces a deeply hidden belief that you're in some way broken or not good enough. You don't want others to realize this, so your first instinct is to distance yourself from whatever happened. This usually entails running away from it, or burying it deeply so you can pretend it never happened.

I think of shame as being an emotional mushroom. Fungi doesn't like direct sunlight. It prefers a shady environment. That's the same for shame. It doesn't want you to bring it into the open, because then it would die. It prefers to lie in the darkness, waiting for any chance it can find to resurface, usually when you're least expecting it. Every time it arises, you remember how inadequate you are.

The lower your self-esteem, the easier it is for shame to materialize. When you already believe you're less than you should be, you use that lens to interpret your experiences. As long as you keep shame hidden, it'll thrive. The best way to deal with it is to bring it out into the open.

I've been experimenting with this idea. Is it possible to stop shame in its tracks, simply by choosing to acknowledge and look directly at the source of it? And what better place to start my trial than with my long-time foe, my body image?

I've been ashamed of my figure for most of my life. It didn't fit with the images I was surrounded by when I grew up. The media had me convinced that I needed to look like Twiggy. Being stick thin and flat-chested was the ideal body shape, back in the day. That was never going to be me. Even when I was very slender, I was always curvy.

I'm sure you can relate to looking back at old photos and regretting not appreciating what you looked like. If you've always loved and valued your physical self, think about something else you've judged as not good enough.

I decided the best way to kick this destructive emotion to the curb was to stop hiding myself – from me. I needed to bring what I believed was broken into the light and let it be seen. Not just once, but regularly. It was time to stop behaving as if my body was something to hide. Instead of looking away from the mirror when I stepped in or out of the shower, it was time to lock eyes with my reflection. I wanted to be able to look at myself without the usual lens of criticism.

I added more opportunities to bring my physique out in the open by performing my morning and bedtime routines without anything on. It was uncomfortable at first, but like anything, I got used to it. One morning I was shocked to see the body that was reflected back to me looked different. I no longer saw a woman who was the size of a barn. Instead, I was greeted by someone with a tall, long-limbed build.

I've spent my life looking through a distorted lens. Yes, there are fat deposits and wrinkles, but they don't make me ugly or substandard. They're simply part of me and the choices I've made. My attitude has changed because I was willing to uncover my shame and expose it to the light.

Regardless of what your body looks like, it still deserves to be nurtured and treated with love and respect. You don't have to look like a model to be worthy of admiration and affection. It's time to stop thinking you're broken. You do not need to be fixed. This applies to mental and emotional aspects of you, as well as your physical appearance.

For me, the process was painful initially, but the end result was worth every moment of my suffering as I discovered that the only person I should care about accepting me, is me.

In a Nutshell

You are undoubtedly your harshest critic. It's unlikely anyone else is judging every flaw and concluding you aren't good enough. In the off-chance that someone is, don't worry about it. What they think isn't part of your journey. That's on them.

> ### Small-step Strategy
>
> Treat shame with a strong dose of light. It can only thrive if you hide it in the deep, dark shadows. Remind yourself that the only person you should care about accepting you, is you. Connect more deeply with happiness by practicing acceptance and releasing shame.

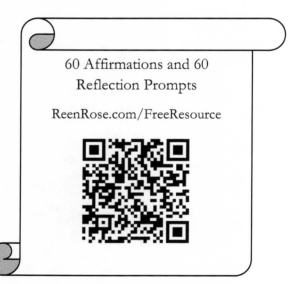

60 Affirmations and 60
Reflection Prompts

ReenRose.com/FreeResource

FIFTY

If You Don't Fall You Can't Get Up

"We don't need to be wise beyond our years. All we need is to be wise beyond our fears."

This is a statement I saw one day when I was scrolling through Facebook. I'm well acquainted with the assertion of being wise beyond one's years. Sometimes the same sentiment is expressed by saying someone's an "old soul." But the idea of being wise beyond one's fears made me pause.

As I compared this statement to the more traditional one, the thing that stood out most was the level of empowerment each one offered. You don't necessarily have control over whether you're wise beyond your years, it's something that's bestowed on you through circumstance and genetic makeup. Being wise beyond your fears, on the other hand, is about conscious choice. That idea appeals to me. It moves you from victim energy to liberation, from being chosen to consciously choosing.

Wisdom involves using knowledge and experiences to make good judgements and decisions. It also involves having a tolerance for the uncertainties of life. If you cling to what's familiar, you may find yourself making decisions that help you avoid the unknown, even if it isn't a wise choice.

How many people stay in relationships or jobs they don't feel good about, or vacation in the same place every year? If that sounds like you, rest assured, you're not alone. This behavior is motivated by fear of the unknown. It encourages you to settle, rather than reach for the stars.

Society has convinced many people that the things they value most, like loving relationships, satisfying jobs, and happiness, are rare. They're limited to a few lucky people. If you believe you aren't one of the fortunate ones, this subconscious belief can encourage you to hang tightly to what you've got. It doesn't matter if you're spending time with people who treat you badly, or in a job that's slowly killing you. At least you have a friend and a pay cheque. It could be worse.

Believing you aren't worthy of anything better than what you presently have can keep you stuck in mediocrity. It's known as a "scarcity mindset" and it isn't only limiting: it can be downright dangerous to your mental health. It's part of a vicious cycle that involves your self-esteem. Low self-esteem causes mental scarcity, which, in turn, teaches you to think less of yourself.

Breaking this cycle is often easier said than done. At the heart of a scarcity mindset is the belief that you don't deserve or can't have more. In order to fight that thought, you need to disprove it. In my experience, the best way to do that is to work towards outcome independence. Outcome independence is exactly what it sounds like. It involves becoming liberated from making decisions based on desired outcomes and instead focusing on the experience that results from your choice.

Like mental scarcity, outcome independence is a mindset. If you believe losing what you have is the worst thing that could happen, you'll put all your time and energy into hanging on to whatever you've got. Your fear of being left with nothing will fuel that fire.

Lots of people are afraid to try something new for fear they'll fail to achieve their desired outcome. Dating without finding the person of your dreams may feel like a waste of time, or even embarrassing. But is it really? Ask yourself: what's the worst thing that can happen? Is still being single after six months or a year of dating the end of the world? Have you actually lost anything? You may make new friends and happy memories as a result.

That doesn't mean the things that happen and the decisions you make won't be difficult, or that they won't leave you feeling hurt or upset. But when you know there are other opportunities out there, it's easier to rebound or change directions.

In a Nutshell

Outcome independence involves realizing you can cope without the things you're afraid of losing. It fosters self-esteem because it helps you realize you can handle whatever comes your way, even if that involves your job or relationships. The only way to truly understand this is to experience it. You need to fall to prove to yourself that you can get up. Once you accept this belief, an abundance mentality is the inevitable result.

Small-step Strategy

If you want to live your best life, take a few minutes to consider whether fear is motivating your decisions. If it is, give outcome independence a try. It might be just what you need to find the wisdom that lives beyond your fear.

FIFTY-ONE

Being Happy Even When It's Elusive

What do you do when happiness seems to elude you? How do you cope when "fine" or "okay" are the best feel-good emotions you can summon? It would be great if emotions were switches you could simply make a choice to turn on or off. In truth, choice is involved, but sometimes it isn't as simple as that.

I consider myself a happiness maven, but I spent time one summer struggling to find joy. One day, when I was feeling particularly low, the wonderful man I share my life with suggested I spend the day doing whatever made me happy. It was great advice. The problem, however, was that I wasn't sure what would make me happy. When a woman who's spent decades studying positive psychology and weaving the eight precepts for happiness into her life feels like she's lost her way, there's a problem.

Life rarely stands still for long. Circumstances change, causing your life to shift and feel unbalanced. When that happens, you may find your level of happiness slumping. Few people are fortunate enough to escape major challenges in their lives. When an unforeseen pit opens in front of you and threatens to swallow you up, what do you do? How can you lift yourself out of a funk that seems to have you fully in its grasp?

I can't give you a definitive solution. But I can help you understand what your brain is doing when your life feels like it's been turned upside down. I can also give you some tips on how to invite a little more joy into it.

The major drive for all humans is to survive. When you feel uncertain about the world around you, your brain puts you into survival mode. In that state, you'll feel hypersensitive to anything that could possibly be perceived as a threat. You're on the lookout for things that might go wrong, even if the likelihood is slim. Rather than giving others the benefit of the doubt, you may find yourself reading negativity into their words and actions. Your fight/flight/freeze response is ready to kick in at a moment's notice.

You may feel a sense of safety, but feeling safe isn't the same as being happy. In fact, the sense of having survived the day without any major mishap can reinforce prioritizing surviving over thriving.

I spent much of that unhappy summer doing just that. Even though both my kids came for a visit from England with their partners, something was missing. Rather than wringing every drop of happiness out of each day, my brain was focused on keeping me safe. I enjoyed my summer, but not to its fullest.

So, what do you do when you find yourself in a situation like that? To be truly happy, you need to find a way to rise above survival mode. You want to feel like you're thriving, not just surviving.

Here are four steps to help you.:

Use the wisdom of the Dalai Lama

The purpose of living is to be happy. It's a major factor in good mental and physical health.

Set an intention at the start of every day

"Today's going to be full of joy."

"I'm going to have an amazing day."

"No matter what happens, I'm going to find lots of reasons to laugh."

Your brain's designed to find examples that support whatever objective you choose. That's why deciding you're going to get through the day unscathed isn't the right attitude to embrace if you want to rise out of survival mode.

Smile, smile, smile

Any time you can, form your lips into the biggest grin possible. When you smile, even if it's forced, your brain releases "feel good" chemicals. These encourage you to smile even more, boosting your happiness further. Remind yourself to smile every chance you get.

Find reasons to laugh

Laughter really is the best medicine when it comes to happiness and to health.

Norman Cousins, an American political journalist, author, professor, and world peace advocate, believed he cured himself of an illness that doctors were unable to help with by watching movies that made him laugh. His research showed that the physical movement that occurs when you laugh moves lymph fluid around your body and helps clear toxins. It also increases the amount of oxygen in your cells and decreases the stress hormone cortisol.

This isn't an exhaustive list of ways to lift yourself out of survival mode, nor does it guarantee your life will stop sucking. But if the Dalai Lama is right and the purpose of life is to be happy, it's a good place to start.

In a Nutshell

Positive emotions release key neurotransmitters like endorphins, dopamine, and serotonin. These are your natural painkillers, mood boosters, and antidepressants. Being in a state of survival long-term doesn't serve your physical or mental health, so it's worth your time and energy to do what it takes to step away from that mind space.

Small-step Strategy

If you want to strengthen your happiness connection at a moment's notice, create a library of resources so you aren't frantically searching for something to make you laugh when you realize you haven't chuckled for hours. Create a collection of books, social media posts, television shows, movies, family photos, etc. that make you laugh. Surround yourself with them and schedule time to focus on them. Make sure you have at least one deep belly laugh every day.

FIFTY-TWO

Take a Step Back From Yourself

*Distancing: make (someone or something) far off or remote
in position or nature.*

Oxford Languages

You're probably well acquainted with the term "social distancing," but have you ever encountered "psychological distancing"? Psychological distancing refers to the process of stepping away from people or situations to gain perspective. It's something that can benefit your health and is probably a term we should all get used to.

Knowing how to achieve psychological distance is especially helpful if the person you need some space from is yourself; more specifically, that voice in your head that loves to share its opinions. The monologue it spouts comes from a combination of your conscious thoughts and personal beliefs and biases.

If you suffer from low self-esteem, this voice is likely to be critical and will delight in reminding you of your shortcomings and perceived weaknesses.

"You're too fat to ever find someone to love and desire you."

"Don't bother applying for that job. They'll never give it to someone like you."

"Why spend all that time getting ready when nobody's going to want to talk to you anyway? You might as well just stay home."

These may sound familiar, or it may be something else that your inner voice loves to whisper in your ear when you least desire it. Having a low opinion about yourself can impact your physical and mental wellbeing. Poor self-esteem can ruin your ability to connect with others, rob you of happiness, or sabotage your career.

It's important to understand that, just because your inner voice is telling you negative things about yourself, that doesn't mean any of it's true. When your self-talk becomes critical, take a step back. Give yourself psychological distance.

Psychologist Ethan Kross, the author of *Chatter: The Voice in Our Head, Why It Matters, and How to Harness It* (2022), discovered that gaining perspective by giving yourself space is a powerful way to silence negative self-talk. An easy way to do this is to simply change your inner responses from first person pronouns to third person. When your inner chatter suggests you aren't good enough to get a promotion, instead of responding, "Yes I am," try, "Yes she is." This approach creates space. It's like referring to a friend or family member.

Try this technique with a limiting belief you hold about yourself.

"Carrying around a few extra pounds doesn't mean she isn't loveable."

"Just because she didn't go to university doesn't mean she isn't intelligent."

"She's good enough to do whatever she decides to do."

Research shows that using a high percentage of "I-talk," or first-person singular pronouns, is a reliable marker of negative emotions. It keeps you too closely attached to the feelings you're experiencing. Talking in the third person lets you take a valuable step back.

Another simple yet effective technique you can use to combat negative self-talk is to refer to yourself by name.

When my inner voice makes negative comments, I've started asking myself, "Is that really true, Reen?" Using my name puts me into a position of separation, as if I'm talking about one of my children. It helps reframe my inner thoughts in more abstract and less emotional terms.

This isn't a new technique. The following quotes are from *Meditations*, by the stoic Roman emperor, Marcus Aurelius.

"You have power over your mind — not outside events.
Realize this, and you will find strength."

"If you are distressed by anything external, the pain is not
due to the thing itself, but to your estimate of it; and this
you have the power to revoke at any moment."

It may sound like he's addressing his readers, but the Meditations are his private notes to himself. These extracts also demonstrate another effective tool for combating negative self-talk: consciously add third person positive affirmations to your inner conversations.

"Her beauty shines from the inside out."

"She is strong enough to do anything she puts her mind to."

"Anyone would be lucky to have her for a friend."

Psychological distancing can give you the healing space you need to view your negative self-talk more realistically. Stepping back gives perspective and allows you the opportunity to make better decisions and to respond in a more appropriate manner. So, the next time the voice in your head needs to be silenced, start by giving yourself some space.

In a Nutshell

Talking about yourself in the third person allows you to step back from emotions that come with negative self-talk. That means using he/she/they/it rather than I/we in your sentences. Gaining greater perspective makes it easier to see the truth about the things your inner voice is telling you.

> ### Small-step Strategy
>
> When you notice negative self-talk, respond in the third person as if the words are aimed at somebody else.
>
> *"She is not fat!"*
>
> Then create an affirmation around it.
>
> *"My body is strong, healthy, and uniquely beautiful!"*

FIFTY-THREE

Know How You're Feeling

Humans are programed to pay more attention to problems than to the things that make them happy. It's part of your drive to survive. It's also one of the reasons why you may notice tough times more than good ones.

In more primitive times, ignoring a threat frequently resulted in death. Today's threats are more likely to be annoying than life-threatening, but that reality doesn't change your internal coding. Your brain reacts to anything it perceives as dangerous with the fight/flight/freeze response. Your mind may think it's serving you with this reaction, but focusing on negative things can lower your level of happiness.

Evidence-based research shows numerous benefits attached to feeling good about yourself and your life. They include a greater level of success, better health, and stronger personal connections. Assessing your level of happiness can be tricky because it's a very subjective thing. If you aren't sure whether you spend more time considering your positive or negative emotions, try this simple exercise.

1. Think about a situation that was emotionally difficult. This will serve as inspiration for step two.

2. Write down all the negative emotions you can think of.

3. Recall a positive experience.

4. Make a list of positive emotions.

5. Add up the number of words on each list.

If you can name negative emotions effortlessly, but struggle to think of positive ones, it's likely you're giving more attention to the former type of feelings. That isn't unusual if you consider humans are coded to unconsciously scan the environment for threats.

If your positive emotions list is long, congratulations. Keep up the good work.

Drawing your brain's attention to a wider range of emotions can broaden your emotional vocabulary. Don't just stick to the positive ones. It's equally beneficial to realize you're exhausted, seething, or resentful. Naming your negative emotions takes their emotional charge away. It also allows you to make a choice about what you want to do with them.

Rather than wondering why you're feeling the way you are, simply acknowledge that's how you're feeling. That makes it less likely you'll have an emotional outburst. You can't change or let go of something you don't notice. Before I understood this, there were times in my life when feelings of frustration and irritation lingered for days, coloring my life a sad shade of blue.

Don't wait for your emotions to demand your attention through a meltdown or temper tantrum. By simply choosing to accurately name how you're feeling on a regular basis, you can change your life for the better. So, stop right now and ask yourself, "How are you...really?"

In a Nutshell

Drawing your brain's attention to a wider range of emotions can broaden your emotional vocabulary. Don't just notice your feelings when they're screaming at you, check in with them regularly. Pause and ask yourself the simple question: "How am I feeling?"

> ### Small-step Strategy
>
> I recommend setting a reminder on your phone, or asking yourself how you are every time you have a cup of tea or coffee, or whenever you take a bathroom break. Find the most honest and accurate words to describe your emotions at that moment. If you want to expand your vocabulary, research more words using the internet or a thesaurus.

FIFTY-FOUR

Focus

Have you been brainwashed into believing that being able to multi-task is important for your success? I grew up being told that women were particularly good at this skill, but new research shows that if you want to make big strides toward your chosen goals, multi-tasking is not your friend.

No one can actually do two things at the same time, unless one of them requires absolutely no brain power. Rather than doing several tasks simultaneously, multi-taskers switch their brain power from one task to another repeatedly. If you're trying to listen to someone while you're reading an email, you might read a few words, then listen to a few words, then read a few words... You get the idea.

That may work for a short period of time, if luck is with you, but the minute both tasks need your attention at the same time, you're in trouble.

Regardless of how good you are at switching your brain from one task to another, research shows that you'll be more efficient and produce better quality work if you concentrate on one task at a time. Believe me when I say that pausing your task to take a phone call, and resuming it when the call has been completed, will produce a much better phone call and completed task than trying to talk while you type, calculate, or help the kids with their homework.

If you struggle to stick with one task at a time, here are some tips to help you focus:

- Eliminate known distractions.

- Only check your email and social media posts at certain times of the day.

- Turn off all your notifications so you don't get distracted by pop ups and envelope icons.

- Turn off your phone and find a place to work where you won't be distracted. Of course, this might not be possible for your particular type of work, but if you can, do it.

- Write down and prioritize your tasks and then get your must-do tasks done first. This organization will take pressure off your day. You may love time pressure, but give this method a try. You might be surprised at its efficiency.

- Pause to think before you say yes. Is the request you're receiving going to move you closer to your end goals? Is it something you are interested in, or feel would be a good experience for you to have? Do you feel moved to get involved? If the answer to these questions is no, say no.

With these tips in mind, you may stop feeling there just aren't enough hours in a day.

In a Nutshell

Being busy with tasks that are just distractions will slow you down more than anything else. Busyness is not a productive strategy for success. If you get focused, your days will seem longer – in a good way – because it'll seem like you have time to get stuff done.

Small-step Strategy

Set an intention to stop multi-tasking. This will help you increase your awareness of this behavior. When you notice yourself trying to do more than one thing at a time, pause. Choose one task to complete and put the other ones in a queue. If another person's involved, it's okay to explain that you need to finish what you're doing first, so you can give them your full attention. Then keep to your word and don't let yourself become distracted.

FIFTY-FIVE

Have an Open Mind

Are you open-minded?

Open-mindedness is the willingness to find and consider a variety of perspectives, values, opinions, or beliefs, even if they contradict your personal convictions. If you answered my opening question with yes, it might surprise you to discover that, unless you're being very conscious and deliberate about seeking out other perspectives, you might not be as open-minded as you think.

Your brain can't possibly process all the information it receives. The majority of data is stored in your subconscious. How does your mind decide what to make you aware of? Things that are important to you, fit with your values, or that you've been thinking about recently determine what your brain sends to your conscious mind. Anything that doesn't fit tends to be ignored.

With that in mind, it's easy to see why you may fall victim to your mind's good intentions and think what it draws your attention to is all that exists. It's important to understand that there's a plethora of contradictory information out there that your mind isn't sharing with you.

But that's not the only reason to cultivate an open mind. Research shows being curious about other viewpoints, and actively looking for evidence that contradicts your current thinking, comes with more benefits than simply seeing and accepting other perspectives more easily. Open-minded people have been found to be healthier, happier, more creative, mentally stronger, and more tolerant. They also achieve a greater level of personal growth and are more optimistic and resilient.

If you aren't sure just how open-minded you are, try this exercise.

1. Choose a contentious issue that you have an opinion about. It could be same-sex marriages, taxing the rich to give to the poor, electric cars, or any other issue that has multiple perspectives.

2. At the top of one piece of paper write, FOR. On another, write AGAINST. List all the reasons you can think of to support your opinion, and then all the things that back an alternate view.

3. Look at the two lists. Are they similar in length? If you have lots of reasons to support your view and few to back an opposite perspective, it may be time to open your mind a little more.

4. Spend time leveling up the length of the two lists. You may need to do some research to achieve this. Remember not to judge. This is about accepting the possibility of other perspectives having validity, not deciding what's right and what's wrong.

If you need more practice, choose another topic, and repeat the exercise. Doing this regularly will help you become more deliberate and conscious about opening your mind to other viewpoints. No one is asking you to change what you believe unless it feels like that's the right thing to do. It's about being able to accept the merits of different ideas instead of dismissing them as worthless.

Start looking for middle ground in your beliefs and opinions, rather than hanging on to extremes. Make a list of polar opposite words like right/wrong, good/bad, happy/sad, etc. For each pair, think of at least one word that would come in the grey zone between them. Bonus points if you can find multiple words. For example, between black and white lies grey, peppery, ash, and dusky.

It turns out that open-mindedness is also an accurate predictor of workplace success. Being more accepting of other perspectives not only contributes to a more harmonious business environment, it also improves your judgements and decisions. When people in leadership positions have open minds, they're better at looking for creative solutions and at turning to members of their team for advice.

It's not about being right; it's about finding the best solution. If you want to encourage colleagues to be more open-minded, avoid arguing and instead be respectful of all viewpoints. You don't want anyone to feel defensive. Ask questions that encourage them to reflect on their own beliefs and on alternative viewpoints. Help them to understand that it isn't a conversation about right and wrong.

In a Nutshell

In an increasingly polarized world, the ability to view yourself, your environment, and the people around you with an open mind is becoming increasingly important. It's the key to morphing our ever-shrinking, multicultural world into one that's more unified and collaborative.

Everyone has a bias towards thinking their beliefs are right, but that doesn't mean you can't override that programing.

Small-step Strategy

Consciously and deliberately add one of the following ideas into your life. When you feel comfortable with your chosen activity, choose another one. These make great journal topics.

- Actively look for multiple perspectives.

- Practice thinking outside your own box.

- Reflect on your beliefs and points of view. Challenge them. Beliefs are highly personal, and sometimes you aren't even aware they exist.

- Use meditation or breathing exercises to encourage a state of calmness, so you don't become angry with people who are different from you.

- Surround yourself with open-minded, positive people.

- Step out of your comfort zone regularly.

Small-step Strategy Continued

- Be okay with having your ideas challenged.

- Consider what others are thinking, without judging them.

- Be willing to accept that the way you do things isn't the only way, nor will it always be the best way.

- Be open to possibility.

- Be curious.

- Release the need to judge yourself or others.

FIFTY-SIX

Live Life for Today

Thinking about the future can be a source of both excitement and stress. I'm currently making some big changes in my life and I'm experiencing the entire spectrum of emotions. Will things work out? Maybe not. Will I wish I'd made different choices? Probably. It's impossible to know what's going to happen tomorrow.

Research shows that thinking about yourself in the future lights up the same parts of the brain as when you think about someone other than yourself. This suggests you don't really consider your future self to be you. It's a stranger that may or may not be the person you eventually become.

When you imagine yourself in the years to come, you probably think you'll enjoy doing the same things you do now, and that you'll have identical values and beliefs. But are you the same person you were twenty years ago? If you changed in the last twenty years, why wouldn't you continue to evolve in the next twenty?

I think we would all agree that the development process slows as you age. Children seem to change from one minute to the next, while you might see only minimal differences in an adult from year to year. It's true that the speed of growth slows, but not as much as most people think. The tendency to believe you've experienced significant growth up until this point, but won't grow or mature substantially in the future, is known as the End of History Illusion.

This comes partially because you find it much easier to remember the past than to imagine the future. You mistakenly believe that things that are hard to imagine are unlikely to happen. Being unable to imagine something shows an inability to imagine, not that it's unlikely to happen. Believing you'll be this version of yourself for the rest of your life is common. Research shows at every age, people underestimate how much they'll change in the years to come.

The choices I'm making now will impact my future. But there's no guarantee I'm even going to want the future that I'm currently imagining for myself. Squirreling away money every month from your paycheck so you can spend long days on the beach or golf course may not be something you're interested in doing by the time you reach retirement. Buying a big house for grandchildren who are yet to materialize, or imagining a future crossing off the items on your current bucket list, can be a mistake.

As you agonize over decisions, knowing they'll affect your future, remember that your future self may not appreciate the sacrifices you're making for them today. Rather than trying to please yourself in the future, live in the moment and cross things off your list today.

"Human beings are works in progress that mistakenly think they're finished. The person you are right now is as transient, fleeting, and as temporary as all the people you've ever been. The one constant in our life is change," says Daniel Gilbert in his TED Talk, *The Psychology of Your Future Self*.

Finding happiness involves recognizing this truth. Regardless of what stage of life you're in, you're far from being the final version of you. That won't happen until you take your last breath. Once you grasp this idea, let go of believing that the person you are today can satisfy your future self. Think of all the decisions you made when you were younger that you can only shake your head at. There's no reason to believe things will be any different between your present and future selves.

In a Nutshell

Remind yourself that life is meant to be lived today. This is an important realization if you want to create a stronger happiness connection. Although it's important to consider your future, don't make major sacrifices right now with the mistaken belief that your future self will thank you.

Small-step Strategy

Change is inevitable. Making peace with this fact will have more impact on your life than meticulously planning your future, believing you know what will be best for a version of you that hasn't even materialized yet.

FIFTY-SEVEN

Let Go of the Past

During the last thirty years, I've painted the walls of many rooms. The best results come when I take the time to fill holes and cracks, sand uneven sections, and make sure the surfaces are clean before I start decorating. The principle of prepping before painting applies to many things, including happiness.

Getting stuck in negative memories and/or emotions is a common affliction. It's not only painful, but it also keeps you from moving forward and finding a sense of peace and contentment. If I go back to the decorating analogy, you can't paint or paper over cracks and expect them to vanish permanently. They need to be filled and sanded if you want a good, long-lasting result. Wanting to be happy without addressing emotionally charged experiences that keep surfacing is futile. It's a little like putting a Band-Aid on a severed limb.

It's difficult to be positive when you're consumed with guilt, regret, or bitterness. There's nothing you can do to change what's already happened. You may very well have been treated badly or misunderstood, but it makes no difference. You can't change the past. The only way forward is to let all your outrage and negativity go. History can't be changed.

> *"Resentment is like drinking poison and waiting for the other person to die."*
>
> Saint Augustine

Think about that for a minute. Who's having sleepless nights and is consumed with anger? It's unlikely to be the person you feel aggrieved with. They've probably forgotten all about the situation and moved on. All you're doing by holding onto these feelings is hurting yourself. Negative emotions won't change what happened. They're more likely to keep you stuck and prevent you from moving forward.

Waiting for other people to admit they "did you wrong" isn't a productive way of spending your life. You might think it'll make you feel better, but will it really? Is it worth the suffering you're causing yourself right now?

It's important to remember that your happiness rests on your shoulders, not anyone else's. This other person isn't holding you back, you are. If you want to be happy when you're caught up in a situation like this one, the best way forward is to let your thoughts and feelings go.

That said, letting go isn't always as easy as it sounds. Many humans find it difficult to release beliefs, feelings, and possessions, even though they're no longer serving any positive purpose. It's as if you don't know who you are without them. But believe me, once you let go, the feeling of relief can be life-changing. I know this from personal experience.

It doesn't matter why you're angry or resentful. Accept your emotions for what they are. You don't need reasons or proof to support them.

My favourite tool when it comes to releasing resentment, anger, and bitterness is forgiveness. Forgiving doesn't mean you have to forget what happened, but it removes the emotional charge that's holding you back. I find writing forgiveness letters is amazingly helpful. Don't worry. You don't have to share your words with anyone else. This is about you, and only you.

Forgive the people who caused you so much angst.

Forgive the people who seemed to stand by without coming to your aid.

Forgive yourself for wasting so much of your life being consumed by these events instead of being happy.

Write the letters, read them over, and then either burn or shred them. This last step symbolizes your decision to release through forgiveness.

I like to use the Ho'oponopono prayer to structure my letters. I add how I'm feeling to each of these statements.

I'm sorry

Please forgive me

I love you

Thank you

Remember to write a letter to yourself. Take responsibility for your actions and emotions. Recognize that you didn't have to hang onto your baggage, and forgive yourself for doing it. Keep writing letters as layers of resentment surface. If you've been hanging onto these emotions for months, years, or possibly even decades, you can't expect them to disappear in one day.

Once you start forgiving the past, consciously increase your level of gratitude for the present.

- Keep a gratitude journal.

- Every night before you go to sleep, think of three things you're grateful for that happened that day.

- Set a timer on your phone. When it goes off, stop, and think about something you're grateful for at that moment.

- Deliberately look for gratitude in everything. Surround yourself with it.

Rather than trying to paper or paint over the cracks in your life, take time to do some inner work. Just like redecorating, you'll get a far better result if you do.

In a Nutshell

I believe everything that happens in life benefits all who are affected by it. Some things can be devastating, but they come with hidden blessings if you're willing to look for them. Growth and resilience come from challenges. Be grateful for the tough times, even if they aren't fun to experience.

Small-step Strategy

If you want to be happy and love yourself, but struggle to let go of the past, I recommend you try the above actions. You may find it difficult to do this work by yourself. Don't hesitate to contact a counselor or coach if you need assistance. They can help you if you get stuck or need support.

FIFTY-EIGHT

Doing Things Differently

've been talking about the importance of embracing change for a long time. I even gave my TEDx talk on why humans resist change.

We all have outdated programing that causes us to prefer what we're comfortable with over the unknown. If you like to stay in your comfort zone, you're simply leaning into your ancient coding.

My parents took this approach when home computers became commonplace. Although they were probably about the same age I am now, they decided they were too old to learn something new. Computers were not for them.

Ten years later, they realized avoidance was not the right path. They bought a Mac and began the education process. Being a decade older made learning a new technology more difficult, especially as they weren't used to taking on new skills. Can you relate?

Our ancient ancestors only changed when they were forced into it. Trying something new back then was a dangerous practice. If the new tool or technique didn't work, you were very likely to die. Although that's no longer the case, we continue to carry that same programing.

The only way to hack your existing code is to be aware it exists and then to challenge it when it appears.

If you want to become more comfortable with change, add nimbleness to your list of skills. Merriam-Webster defines nimble as "being quick and light in motion." It is a proactive word. You don't just try to maintain balance; you move in ways that allow you to take advantage of what's happening.

If you want to be nimble, here are five skills to be mindful of.

Be adaptable

Practice doing things differently. Choose routines and habits that serve you and let go of the ones that have been hanging around for no reason. If breaking away from the familiar is stressful, find a small step that doesn't seem too scary and start there. Better to dip your toe into the pond of the unknown daily than to plunge in once and never get wet again. Work your way up to submersing yourself completely in new behaviors.

Know yourself from the inside out

Your brain is adept at giving you the information it thinks you need. Humans are complex. Unless you consciously choose to take a journey of self-discovery, you may never know your genuine self. Confidence comes from trusting yourself. Trust comes from knowing, accepting, and loving who you are, not who you think you should be. If you trust yourself, you will find it easier to welcome new experiences.

Be creative

Creativity fosters good problem solving. When you experience something for the first time, you can't predict everything that will happen. Situations will arise that need to be handled with a different solution.

Find time every day to do something creative. This will help prepare your brain for the unexpected. You have opportunities to be creative in every area of your life. It doesn't necessarily mean visual arts. Work on math problems, write a blog or story, add an organizer to your closet, redecorate your home, cook. The possibilities for creativity are endless.

Let go of limitations

*"Whether you think you can, or you think you can't —
you're right."*

Henry Ford

This famous quote is spot on. You probably have limiting beliefs that you aren't even aware of. This leads back to the importance of point number two: You need to know you have limitations before you can let them go. Delve deeply to discover your authentic self, not the one society and your upbringing has helped you create.

Don't let unexpected outcomes stop you

Rarely, if ever, does any great discovery or innovation happen without setbacks. Don't give up. Keep trying until you are satisfied with what you have accomplished.

In a Nutshell

Nimble isn't a word you hear very often. It reminds me of the nursery rhyme about Jack being nimble. I was curious to know what jumping over the candle stick meant.

Candle jumping was a traditional activity at markets and fairs in England. If you could jump over the candle without putting out the flame, it was a sign of good luck.

Some people may look at nimble people and think they're lucky. I believe you make your luck and nimbleness is one way to help you do that.

Small-step Strategy

On a scale of one to ten, with ten being the most, how nimble are you?

Using the skills listed above, what's one thing you can do to increase your score?

What's one way you can add that skill to your daily life?

Last reminder, I promise!

Get an Affirmation and a Reflection Prompt to go with each chapter.

ReenRose.com/FreeResource

FIFTY-NINE

Create a Self-care Plan

One day, when I was ordering a beverage at my favourite coffee shop, the barista asked me how my week was going. I paused and said it was a strange one. I'm not a proponent of saying "fabulous" unless that's the truth. She laughed and said hers was "off." I gave her a knowing smile as I realized her word described my week perfectly.

What does a happiness maven do when she's feeling low or off her game? She sinks into some self-care by writing in a beloved environment. There's something about the energy of a coffee shop that soothes my soul.

What one person considers nourishing for their body and soul varies widely. It might be a day at the spa, a challenging hike, or time with a book. It's important to not only know what helps when you need an energy reset, but to commit to doing it.

It turns out that there are some vital, yet often ignored, aspects of self-care that don't get as much airtime as things like exercise, eating healthily, and a good night's sleep. Rather than sticking to the usual suspects, consider the following list.

Get help when you need it

Asking for help is often interpreted as a sign of weakness. It isn't. It also doesn't have to mean therapy. It could mean hiring someone to clean your house, finding someone to look after your kids for a few hours, or using a delivery service for your groceries.

If you're asking a friend or family member for help, make sure you know exactly what you need and then be specific about your request. Remember, although you have the right to ask for help, the other person has just as much right to refuse. If that happens, try not to take it personally. Their reasons for declining quite likely have nothing to do with you. Don't let rejection stop you from asking someone else.

Set boundaries

There's nothing wrong with saying no.

That's the flip side of asking for help. If the request doesn't fit with what's happening in your world, or it doesn't feel right, it's okay to refuse. If a friend asks you for a favor that's going to cause you stress, you have every right to say no.

Don't feel you have to justify your decision or explain your refusal. If it seems appropriate, you can offer an alternative way of helping your friend.

Look for a win-win, not a win-lose solution. Helping someone is about believing it's the right thing to do, not obligation. The more you create healthy boundaries, the easier it gets.

Avoid avoidance

If you have something hanging over your head, demanding your attention, you'll find it difficult to feel truly free. The closer you get to a deadline, the heavier the task is likely to feel. If you love to put things off, do one thing to get started on the task at hand. You don't have to get the whole thing done in one fell swoop. Break the project into small steps and give yourself a pat on the back every time you complete even a tiny bit of the task.

Release perfection

Sometimes a "good enough" attitude serves you more than a perfectionist one. Stop overthinking stuff that really doesn't matter. Ask yourself if you'll care about how well it was done in a week, month, or year.

It's taken me more time than I care to admit to accept that people come to visit me, not to see a clean and tidy home.

Mind your money

While money can't buy happiness, it can provide you with peace of mind. Creating a budget and sticking to it may be one of the greatest gifts you give yourself. If necessary, ask for help to educate yourself about your finances.

Declutter

Getting rid of "stuff" has been proven to reduce stress, increase productivity, aid decision-making, and increase brainpower. It minimizes distractions and allows you to focus on what's really important.

You don't have to do your entire home at once. Start with your workspace or bedroom, and when that's done, choose the next area you want to tackle. If a whole room seems too daunting, begin with a single drawer or cupboard. If this is an area you feel particularly challenged with, reach out to a decluttering specialist. Remember, asking for help is just another type of self-care.

Put free time or "me time" on your calendar

It's important to schedule time for yourself. Don't wait for it to magically appear, because that rarely happens. Set boundaries around it and refuse to sacrifice it for anything less than an emergency.

In a Nutshell

Your energy requires regular maintenance, even when your life seems to be going well. Don't wait for things to be "off" before you take steps to rejuvenate yourself. Research shows ignoring your personal needs contributes to exhaustion, career setbacks, burnout, lower self-esteem, less money, and shaky mental health. These make it more difficult to connect with happiness.

Small-step Strategy

If you don't know how to care for yourself in times of need, create a plan. If you're already a self-care guru, consider adding some or all of these less-common ways of taking care of yourself, into your regime.

If you aren't sure where to begin, look at your daily routine and ask yourself, "What's one small thing I can do every day that will make me feel happier, healthier, or more at peace?" Schedule it into your life and make it a priority.

SIXTY

Practice Happiness

Are you happy? I'm not asking whether life could be worse, or if you're grateful for what you've got. I want you to think about whether you're happy. Pause, close your eyes, and focus on the question. You may discover that choosing yes or no is more complicated than it might appear at first glance. Don't rush to find an answer. Accept what comes to mind and then dig a little deeper, focusing purely on the query: are you happy?

Thoughts that might run through your mind could include:

What is happiness?

I felt happy 10 minutes ago, but now I'm irritated. This question is irritating.

I have such a great life; it feels wrong to say I'm not happy.

I don't feel happy, but I don't feel unhappy, either.

This isn't a test. There isn't a right answer. The purpose of this exercise is to help you look more closely at your feelings and what you believe about your life. Awareness is vital in any area of growth. That's true whether you're striving to progress in your personal life or at work. You don't know whether something needs tweaking, overhauling, or to be left as is, until you know what the current state of play is. If you want to make changes to how you feel about your life, self-awareness and total honesty are two major keys to success.

Happiness is an emotion, but it's also a state of mind. I believe being happy is more about how you approach life, not the ever-present feelings of joy and excitement. Some days you may feel grumpy or irritated. On others, you may find tears close to the surface. That doesn't mean you aren't a happy person. Being happy is about your approach to life and how you react to challenges, and disappointments. It requires constant and consistent monitoring. When you practice happiness, you don't expect to love every moment of your life. But when challenges appear, you aren't surprised, nor do you expect them to last forever.

I practice happiness regularly and, generally speaking, am a pretty contented and positive person. However, with recent occurrences in my life, I've had to remind myself of some of the principles that are instrumental to the practice of happiness, like:

- I am solely responsible for my own happiness. Others may bring joy and pleasure, but without them, I am still capable of being happy.

- I'm not responsible for how other people view life, or whether they're happy. That's their responsibility.

- Practicing happiness doesn't mean I'll never experience negative emotions. All feelings should be acknowledged and accepted. They serve different purposes. My task is to understand their message and then choose to keep them or let them go. Everyone who's touched by an event or challenge has the same opportunity for growth, though not necessarily in the same way. Whether you capitalize on it or not is up to you.

With these principles firmly in my mind, I'm ready to get back to being happy.

In a Nutshell

Happiness doesn't come from what happens to you. It springs from the choices and decisions you make. You get to choose your reaction, perspective, and next steps. There's more than one perspective to everything. You have the power to choose the way you want to view your life.

Small-step Strategy

Try to recall the last time you experienced a negative emotion. Was there a cause? How did you react? Was there anything you could have done differently?

Parting Words of Wisdom

Reflection: Consideration of some subject matter, idea, or purpose.

Merriam-Webster Dictionary

A dults learn through the process of reflection. If you want to experience more happiness, contentment, satisfaction, or other positive emotions, it's vital that you take time to consider the wisdom contained in these pages. You don't have to agree with it all or absorb it into your life. Embrace the things that resonate and release anything that doesn't speak to you. Please share anything you feel would benefit someone else.

You may not find the same result if you simply read the book without reflecting or incorporating the ideas, but that doesn't mean it won't be useful. You'll still be providing your brain with a wealth of information that it can use to support you on your journey.

Remember:

- Embrace possibility over limitation. Miracles happen when you open your mind beyond what seems probable. By believing in the potential for positive change and maintaining a mindset focused on growth and opportunity, you can invite more miracles into your life.

- Extreme emotions are fleeting although it may not seem that way at the time.

- Let go of perfectionism and societal expectations. Instead, embrace imperfections and scars. This will help encourage personal growth and resilience.

- Consciously choose a path of self-discovery, acceptance, and authenticity. This will help you navigate uncertainties and new experiences with grace and confidence.

- Long journeys are made up of small steps. Don't think you can change your world in a few days. It takes time. By using a Small-step Strategy, you can achieve huge changes. The secret is just to get started.

- Happiness starts from the inside. It isn't about your possessions or circumstances, but how you view those things. It's about getting to know your authentic self, accepting it, and choosing to grow daily. This is where the power of practicing happiness comes from.

Regardless of what's happening in your world, you have the ability to practice happiness and to reap the resulting benefits.

I wish you every success as you travel this road, regardless of whether you're new to the journey or a seasoned adventurer. It may not always be easy, but strengthening your happiness connection will be consistently rewarding and satisfying. Good luck and safe travels.

Acknowledgements

As always, writing a book and getting it published is never a solo accomplishment. I may be the one who sat down to put words on paper, but that's only one part of this project. Many wonderful people gave me their support and encouragement. I appreciate all of you.

Because the contents of this book are based on my column for Castanet.net, I want to start by acknowledging the man who got me started. Eight years ago, Ross Freake was the columns editor. He approached me about writing a weekly column. I thought about it for some time before I agreed, and *The Happiness Connection* was born. More than three hundred submissions, 1.5 million views, and two editors later, I've honed my craft more than anything else I could ever have done.

I want to thank all the people who've taken the time to read my work. I always appreciate the emails you send to share your thoughts. They aren't always positive, but I'm grateful you've felt moved enough to reach out.

I want to give a special shoutout to my Editor and Proofreader, Emily Swan. You understood the meaning behind the words and helped me shape them into chapters that made sense. Your ability to notice inconsistencies in formatting continues to amaze me.

The beautiful cover was designed by Sandy Magee at Red Sand Creative. As always, you've taken my ideas and created something amazing.

Geoff Affleck at AuthorPreneur Publishing was my guru for all things publishing related. I'm grateful for how generously he shared his wisdom and expertise.

The headshot was taken during a photoshoot with Kristen at Story Catcher Photography. I came away with so many amazing photos.

Lastly, I want to thank my sweetheart, David Church. You give me the time and space to create, provide me with ideas and experiences to write about, and are always my biggest fan. You make my life better than I thought possible.

About the Author

Reen Rose's life was a positive one, until it wasn't. Her journey into understanding happiness began when she experienced a deep depression in her early thirties. Realizing she lacked the skills to manage her wellbeing, she began delving into evidence-based research. Not only did she want to improve her own life, she was also determined to do everything she could to help her children avoid similar struggles.

As well as being a clinically depressed happiness maven, Reen is a passionate life-long learner, TEDx speaker, author, and the creator of the Modelling Happiness Movement. Her certifications include Microsoft Office Specialist Master Trainer, Myers Briggs Certified Practitioner, and a degree in Education. She and her life-partner live with their two dogs in the Okanagan Valley in British Columbia.

You can find more information about Reen and the services and programs she provides, as well as her social media links, by going to her website at www.ReenRose.com.

Also by Reen Rose

Available from Amazon worldwide.

"Well written, accessible, and full of insights based on the author's experience backed up with research. It is full of practical strategies to help children learn how to be happy and deal with life's ups and downs."

—Gina Gardiner,
Transformational Leadership Coach and
#1 best-selling author of *Thriving Not Surviving*

"Definitely a must read....great strategies...highly recommended."

—Deanne Neufeld, BSW, MSW

Made in the USA
Columbia, SC
27 December 2024

50750706R00145